Collins

Student Support Materials for AQA

AS and A-level

Sociology

Families and Households

Authors: Martin Holborn and Judith Copeland

Published by Collins
An imprint of HarperCollins*Publishers*
The News Building
1 London Bridge Street
London
SE1 9GF

Browse the complete Collins catalogue at
www.collins.co.uk

ISBN 978-0-00-822166-9

British Library Cataloguing in Publication Data.

A catalogue record for this publication is available
from the British Library.

Commissioned by Catherine Martin

Developed by Jo Kemp

Project managed by Sadique Basha at Jouve

Copyedited by Nikky Twyman

Proofread by Lucy Hyde

Original design by Newgen Imaging

Typeset and Indexed by Jouve India Private Limited

Cover design by Ink Tank

Cover image by kosmos111/Shutterstock

Production by Lauren Crisp

Printed and bound by Grafica Veneta S. P. A.

Acknowledgements

Every effort has been made to contact the holders of
copyright material, but if any have been inadvertently
overlooked the publishers will be pleased to make the
necessary arrangements at the first opportunity.

p 15, fig 2, source: ONS; p 29, tables 6 and 7, source:
based on figures from Social Trends 2011; p 32, table 8,
source: based on figures from Social Trends 2011;
p 34, table 9, source: Equality and Human Rights
Commission (2009); p 37, table 10, source: ONS Social
Trends 2009; p 38, fig 7, source: ONS 2016; p 40, fig 8,
source: ONS; p 48, table 12, source: British Social
Attitudes Survey; p 49, table 13, source: ONS Time Use
Survey 2005; p 52, fig 10, source: Home Office (2010)
Crime in England and Wales 2009/10; p 60, fig 11,
source: ONS Social Trends 2009; p 61, fig 12, source:
ONS 2009; p 72, fig 15, source: ONS and www.statistics.
gov.uk

Thanks to Peter Langley for his work as series editor on
the first edition.

Contents

Introduction

At first sight it seems easy to define the family. Most people could easily identify who they consider to be members of their family. Usually this will include their mother and father, brothers and sisters, any children and possibly less close relatives such as grandparents, aunts and uncles. We are connected to these individuals either through blood (genetic) links or through marriage. Seeing the family in this way is a commonsense definition of the family, and this was the starting point for the functionalist sociologist George Peter Murdock (1949).

Murdock defined the family as 'a social group characterized by common residence, economic cooperation and reproduction. It includes adults of both sexes, at least two of whom maintain a socially approved sexual relationship, and one or more children, own or adopted, of the sexually cohabiting adults'.

Murdock studied 250 societies and claimed the family, as defined above, was present in all of them. He therefore saw it as a **universal** institution (found in all societies) which was necessary for the smooth functioning and survival of any society.

Murdock's definition only includes members of the **nuclear family**, which consists of two generations, parents and their immature offspring. The **extended family** also includes relations by blood or marriage from other generations (e.g. grandparents) and the siblings of parents (aunts and uncles of the children) as well as more distant relatives such as cousins.

Is the family universal?

A problem with Murdock's views is that a number of societies have very different domestic arrangements to those he describes. These examples may suggest that the family is not universal.

The Nayar

Research by Kathleen Gough (1959) into the **Nayar** of southern India found that wives did not live with the man they married (their *tali* husband) and instead had several visiting husbands (*sandbanham* husbands). Sandbanham husbands slept with a wife but did not live with her permanently. These husbands (who were usually warriors) would arrive at their wife's house at night but would have to leave if another man had arrived first and had left his spear outside the house. Each man could have several wives. In terms of Murdock's definition this society did not possess a family since fathers did not live with their children.

Matrifocal families

Research in the Caribbean, parts of central America and the USA has found that a significant proportion of households do not contain an adult male. These female-headed or **matrifocal families** appear to be an exception to Murdock's belief that the nuclear family is universal.

The sociologist Gonzalez (1970) found that matrifocal families are a well-organized social group which is well adapted to living in poverty. The mothers who head these families often get strong support from female relatives that helps them to cope with raising children. Yanina Sheeran

Examiners' notes

Definitions are invaluable in exams. On the AS paper there is a 2-mark question asking you to define a term and in longer answers you can often gain credit by defining key terms. It is well worth learning Murdock's definition of the family off by heart and repeating it where appropriate. You should also be able to evaluate it.

Examiners' notes

It is very useful to be able to refer to cross-cultural examples such as those discussed here. If the question does not specify which societies you can discuss, try to use a variety of examples and not just those from Western industrialized societies such as the UK and US. However, do look out for questions that specifically reference Britain, and give British examples for these.

(1993) believes that the **female carer-core**, consisting of a mother and her children, is the basic family unit. She argues that this family unit is universal. However, a problem with this definition is the existence of male-headed households, where a single father raises children.

Gay and lesbian families

Gay families do not conform to Murdock's definition because they do not contain adults of both sexes and in some societies the sexual relationship involved might not be approved throughout society. They might, however, include children from a previous heterosexual relationship, or children who have been adopted or produced through new reproductive technologies. Sydney Callahan (1997) believes that gay or lesbian households with children should be regarded as families.

In 2005 in the UK, **civil partnerships** (which involve similar legal rights and obligations to marriage) for gay and lesbian couples were legalized, implying that gay and lesbian relationships are now socially accepted and their households should be regarded as families. In 2014, laws allowing same-sex marriage came into force.

Conclusion – ideology and the family

As we have seen, there are a range of problems with Murdock's definition of the family. These are summarized below.

Definition	Problem
Common residence	Husband and wife do not always cohabit, e.g. the Nayar
Sexually approved adult relationships	Lack of agreement on approved relationships
Contains adults of both sexes	Lesbian/gay and matrifocal familes do not conform
Contains one or more children	Child-free couples can be seen as a family

Diana Gittins (1993) concludes that there is no single family type that is found in all societies. The form which families and households take varies widely, so it is not possible to produce a definition of the family which fits all societies. Nevertheless, all societies have intimate relationships and parents caring for their children.

Definitions of the family vary and are influenced by ideological differences.

* **New Right** (sometimes known as neoliberal) thinkers tend to support narrow definitions which see nuclear families based around married couples as the only true family type (see p 14). Many supporters of this viewpoint see the family as an institution under threat.
* Increasing family diversity (see p 28) suggests that in countries such as the UK no one type of family is the norm any longer. Supporters of increasing diversity such as the Rapoports (1982) see this as a good thing because it gives people more freedom to choose how to live their lives. From this viewpoint, any household with intimate relationships can be seen as a family.

Examiners' notes

The issue of matrifocal families is also important for discussing family diversity and particularly ethnic diversity.

Examiners' notes

The growth and acceptance of **gay and lesbian families** in some societies is an important aspect of change in families and in society in general.

Table 1
Problems with Murdock's definition of the family

Examiners' notes

The term 'the family' is sometimes used to describe groups living together, usually a nuclear family living under the one roof, but can also be used to describe groups related by blood or marriage who do not live together; for example extended families when the whole family does not share a single residence. Make sure that you specify whether you are describing a co-resident group (or **household**) or not when writing about family types. (A household is a group of people who live together in a single dwelling.)

The functionalist perspective

Functionalists see society as an interrelated whole. To functionalists, every institution in society performs one or more important **functions** or jobs and the sociologist has to determine what these functions are. They assume that institutions help society to run smoothly like a well-oiled machine. Functionalist theories of the family therefore look for the positive benefits and functions the family performs for all societies.

George Peter Murdock – the universal functions of the family

As discussed in on page 4, Murdock (1949) believed that the nuclear family was a universal institution vital to the well-being of all societies. From his study of 250 societies he identified four functions of the family:

1. The **sexual function**. The family prevents disruption to society by limiting sexuality to monogamous relationships, preventing the conflict that might otherwise result from sexual desire.
2. The **reproductive function**. The family ensures the reproduction of a new generation vital for the survival of society.
3. The **economic function**. The family acts as an economic unit ensuring the survival of its members by providing food and shelter.
4. The **educational function**. The family provides a stable environment in which children can be socialized into the culture of their society.

Talcott Parsons – the basic and irreducible functions of the family

Parsons (1959, 1965) studied American society and found that even though the family had lost some functions (see below) it retained two 'basic and irreducible functions':

1. **Primary socialization**. The family was the only institution in which primary socialization (the first and most important stage of socialization) could take place effectively so that children would internalize the norms and values of their society.
2. **Stabilization of adult personalities**. In Western societies the **isolated nuclear family** gets little support from **extended kinship networks**. The stress of the competitive world of work for the husband can be counterbalanced by the warmth and security offered by the nuclear family, and within the family adults can act out the childish elements in their personalities. This helps to stabilize their personalities.

Talcott Parsons – changing family structure

Parsons believed that the structure of the family changes to fit the needs of different types of society.

In **pre-industrial societies** the **extended family** was the norm. Most people worked in agriculture and the extended family worked the land together. The **nuclear family** of parents and children developed in industrial society where it was necessary because:

1. Industry required a geographically mobile workforce which could move to where new factories were being built. This was difficult to achieve with large extended families.

2. A **socially mobile** workforce was also necessary. In extended families, **status** was largely **ascribed** (given by birth) with the eldest males having high status. This could cause problems if younger males had a higher **achieved status** because they had a better job. Nuclear families without extended kin avoided this problem.

Talcott Parsons – changing functions of the family

Parsons argued that as society changes, the family loses some of its functions. In pre-industrial times it carried out many functions but in industrial society specialist institutions take over some of these functions. This process is called structural differentiation.

For example, health care and support for the family used to be the responsibility of the family. Now the **welfare state** has taken over much of the responsibility.

Criticisms of functionalism

The functionalist view of the family has been heavily criticized for being outdated and for presenting an overly optimistic view of family life. Criticisms include the following:

Functionalist view	Criticism
Family has a unique functional role	Some societies don't have traditional families
Family is functional for all members	Ignores 'dark side', e.g. domestic violence, sexual abuse
Family unit benefits all members	Feminists argue men benefit more than women
Families and society benefit from men being main breadwinners and women main carers	Feminists view this as patriarchal and sexist
Dominant family type has shifted from extended to nuclear	Ignores evidence of non-dominance of extended family in the pre-industrial era, and decline of nuclear family and increasing family diversity
Nuclear family best adapted to modern society	Postmodernists argue there are many viable alternatives

Essential notes

The functionalist Ronald Fletcher (1966) believed the family has developed some new functions such as acting as a unit of consumption – goods are bought for families as a whole. Fletcher also believed that the family retains important functions in education and health, supplementing and supporting the job done by schools, doctors and hospitals.

Examiners' notes

All the main perspectives (Marxism, feminism, the New Right/neoliberalism and postmodernism) can be used to criticize functionalism. When revising it is important to identify similarities and differences between the main perspectives. The table of criticisms is not exhaustive; as you work through the material think about other ways that functionalism can be criticized.

Table 2
Criticisms of the functionalist view of family

Introduction to Marxism

According to Marx (1818–83) and Engels (1820–95) power in society largely stemmed from wealth. In particular, those who owned the **means of production** (the things needed to produce other things such as land, capital, machinery and labour power) formed a powerful **ruling class**. They were able to exploit the **subject class** (those who did not own the means of production) and therefore had to work for the ruling class.

Economic systems

According to Marx, society passed through several periods in which different economic systems or **modes of production** were dominant. In each of these there was a different ruling class and subject class. In the latest stage, **capitalist society**, the ruling class were wealthy factory owners (the **bourgeoisie**) and the subject class were the **working-class** employees (the proletariat). In capitalism the proletariat was exploited by the bourgeoisie because they were not paid the full value of their work since the bourgeoisie kept some **surplus value** or profit.

The economic base and superstructure

The power of the bourgeoisie derived from their ownership of the means of production. The means of production formed the **economic base** or infrastructure of society. Because they controlled the economic base the bourgeoisie were able to control the other, non-economic institutions of society (which make up the **superstructure**) such as the media, government, religion and the family.

Examiners' notes

It is important to use technical terms from Marxist theory (such as means of production) when answering exam questions.

Examiners' notes

The economic base/superstructure model of society is very useful for explaining why Marxists see the family as being shaped by the interests of the ruling class.

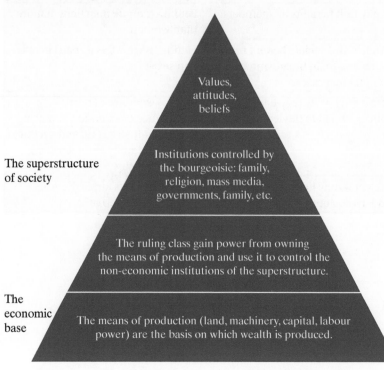

The superstructure of society

Values, attitudes, beliefs

Institutions controlled by the bourgeoisie: family, religion, mass media, governments, family, etc.

The ruling class gain power from owning the means of production and use it to control the non-economic institutions of the superstructure.

The economic base

The means of production (land, machinery, capital, labour power) are the basis on which wealth is produced.

Fig 1
A Marxist model of society

Marxist perspectives on the family

- Engels (1884) argued that the family developed so that men could be certain of the paternity of children, with marriage allowing them to control women's sexuality. This enabled them to be more confident that they were passing their property down to their biological offspring.
- Zaretsky (1976) sees the family as a prop to the capitalist system. The unpaid domestic labour of housewives supports future generations of workers at no cost to capitalist employers. The family consumes the commodities produced by capitalist companies, helping the bourgeoisie to make profits. It also provides comfort to **alienated** workers enabling them to carry on working.
- Poulantzas (1969) sees the family as part of the superstructure of society. He describes it as part of the **ideological state apparatus**, which is controlled by the bourgeoisie and used to create **values**, attitudes and beliefs which support the capitalist system and the position of the ruling class.
- The view of Poulantzas is supported by David Cooper (1972), who sees the family as 'an ideological conditioning device' in which children learn to conform to authority so they will become cooperative and easily exploited workers.

Criticisms of Marxism

The Marxist view of the family has been criticized from a variety of viewpoints.

- Some modern evidence contradicts the view that the family only developed after the herding of animals was introduced.
- Zaretsky has been criticized for exaggerating the extent to which the family can be an escape from alienating work since the family can also be characterized by cruelty, neglect and violence.
- Some families are anti-capitalist and socialize their children into beliefs which are critical of the ruling class.
- Feminists criticize Marxists for neglecting the exploitation of women, postmodernists criticize them for ignoring the variety of family types present in society today and functionalists believe that Marxists ignore the beneficial functions of the family for society.

Strengths of Marxism

Marxism is useful for highlighting the importance of economic influences on family life and because it raises the possibility that the family as an institution benefits some social groups (higher classes) more than others.

Marxism may have been criticized by feminists, but it provided the starting point for Marxist-feminists interested in the economic exploitation of women within the family and in personal relationships. It also provides useful analysis of how broad structural changes in society might have influenced family life.

Examiners' notes

Make sure that you learn the views on the family of at least three Marxists.

Examiners' notes

It can also be useful to discuss Marxist feminist views of the family (see p 12) which are quite similar to Marxist views.

Essential notes

The postmodern view of family life draws attention to the way in which Marxists assume that the nuclear family is still the norm. In fact increasing family diversity (see p 28) raises doubts about the possibility of making any generalizations about the role of families in society.

Examiners' notes

All answers on feminism should use the concept of patriarchy.

The basic principles of feminism

There are several different types of feminist theory, but all of them share certain characteristics in common:

- There is a fundamental division in society between men and women.
- That women are to some extent exploited by men.
- That society is male-dominated or **patriarchal**. Literally, patriarchal means 'rule by the father' but is used by feminists to indicate that men have more power than women and the interests of men largely shape how societies run.

These theories are also all critical of existing sociology, arguing that it has a pro-male bias. They call male-dominated sociology '**malestream**' sociology, claiming that most sociology is written by men, about men and for men. For example, most early studies of the family used all-male samples and paid little attention to women's roles and work within the family such as the role of mother and the work of mothering or housework.

From the early 1970s feminist thinking became more influential in sociology and this was reflected in a growing number of studies of the family from a feminist viewpoint. However, there are important differences between the perspectives of different feminists.

The table below summarizes three of the main varieties of feminism that have been applied to the study of the family.

Examiners' notes

By including different types of feminism in your answer you will tend to get into higher mark bands because you can be given credit for your understanding of theories.

Examiners' notes

If an exam question asks you about Marxist theories of the family, remember that you can include Marxist feminism in your answer as well as conventional Marxism.

	Radical feminism	Marxist feminism	Liberal feminism
Society is controlled by:	Men	Men and capitalists (the wealthy ruling class)	Largely by men who have more power than women, but women do have some power
Society is defined as:	Patriarchal (male dominated)	Patriarchal	Basically democratic but it is also sexist with discrimination against women
Who benefits from inequalities in society?	Men	Men in general, but ruling-class men in particular. Working-class men get wives to work for them (e.g. housework) but the ruling class exploits women both as workers and wives	Nobody. Gender stereotypes mean that men miss out on the private side of life (e.g. raising children) and women miss out in public life, e.g. paid employment

Main ideas behind the theory:	Women are dominated by men due to biology (women give birth, men are stronger) and men use violence or **ideology** (distorted beliefs) to control women	Men's financial power keeps women in their place. Women do more unpaid work (e.g. as mothers and housewives) and receive lower wages making them financially dependent on men	Socialization into gender roles (e.g. differences in boys' and girls' toys) and sexist discrimination (e.g. in the labour market) restrict women's opportunities
Solutions to the exploitation of women:	Radical change (e.g. a female-dominated society or separation of the sexes)	Communist revolution or more economic equality to get rid of men's financial power	Gradual reform. Getting rid of sexism in socialization (e.g. children's books) and the use of language. Laws against discrimination (e.g. Equal Pay Act)
Criticisms:	The idea of patriarchy is too broad and doesn't really explain why women are exploited. It exaggerates the extent of inequality and fails to take account of the development of greater equality	Places too much emphasis on economic factors	Lacks a theory of the underlying causes of inequality

Table 3
Types of feminism

Essential notes

Another criticism that has been made of all these varieties of feminism is that the concept of patriarchy does not really explain gender inequality but only describes it.

Examiners' notes

Remember that the different perspectives can be used to criticize and evaluate one another.

Difference feminism

The three feminist perspectives outlined above all tend to see women as a single group who share interests and are all equally exploited. However, **difference feminism** emphasizes that women are not one single, united group but rather have a variety of interests.

Black feminists, for example, stress the importance of racial/**ethnic** differences between women while other difference feminists emphasize differences in **class**, age or nationality. Difference feminists point out that not all women are equally exploited.

Essential notes

Difference feminism has much in common with postmodernism.

Feminist perspectives and the family

Radical feminism and the family

Radical feminists believe that the family plays a major role in maintaining the oppression of women in a patriarchal, male-dominated society.

Germaine Greer (2000) argues that even in marriage today women remain subservient to their husbands. She believes that single women are generally happier than married women and this is reflected in the high number of divorces instigated by women. Greer claims that wives are much more likely to suffer physical and sexual abuse than husbands, and daughters are often victims of sexual abuse by male relatives within the family.

Marxist feminism and the family

Marxist feminists believe that the family benefits the capitalist system and in doing so exploits women.

- Margaret Benston (1972) claims that wives are used to produce and rear cheap labour for employers. The childcare they provide is unpaid, and they also help to maintain their husbands as workers at no cost to employers.
- Fran Ansley (1972) believes that wives suffer as a result of the frustration experienced by their husbands in the **alienating** work that they do for capitalists.

Liberal feminism and the family

The liberal feminist Jennifer Somerville (2000) believes that women are still disadvantaged in families, but she criticizes radical and Marxist feminists for failing to accept that progress has been made in some ways.

- Women now have much more choice about whether to marry, whether they take paid work when married and whether they stay married.
- There is now greater equality within marriage and greater sharing of the responsibility for paid and unpaid work and childcare.
- Most women still value relationships with men.

However, she agrees there are still inequalities within marriage that need to be tackled through pragmatic reform. For example, better childcare is needed for working parents, and more flexibility is needed in jobs so that both men and women can contribute fully to family life.

Criticisms of radical, Marxist and liberal feminist perspectives on the family

All these perspectives have been criticized for:

- Exaggerating the exploitation of women within the family.
- Largely failing to acknowledge the increasing equality between men and women.
- Oversimplifying by taking little account of differences in the circumstances of different groups of women.
- In particular, not taking account of class, ethnic and age differences.
- Ignoring examples where men are victims of abuse in families.

Functionalists criticize them for failing to acknowledge the positive contribution of the family to society.

Postmodernists criticize them for failing to acknowledge the extent to which society and family life have changed.

Difference feminism and the family

This perspective recognizes that there is increasing family diversity today and women may not be equally exploited in all family types. For example, many women are lone parents and as such cannot be exploited by a cohabiting man. There are also differences in gender relationships in families from different ethnic backgrounds.

- Nicholson (1997) believes that women are often better off outside traditional families and all types of family and household should be socially accepted because they suit women in different circumstances.
- Calhoun (1997) points out that women cannot be exploited by men in lesbian families. She believes that there is increasing choice in family life, and gay and lesbian families are examples of '**chosen families**'.

Criticisms of difference feminism

Difference feminism is not as easy to criticize as other forms of feminism because it recognizes differences in family life. However, other types of feminists criticize it for losing sight of continuing inequalities between men and women within the family.

The contribution of feminism to understanding the family

Despite the criticisms of feminism it has contributed to the sociology of the family in a number of ways:

- It has shown that the family may benefit some members, particularly adult males, more than others.
- It has highlighted the existence of violence, abuse and exploitation within the family.
- Feminists have conducted research into areas of family life which have either been neglected or not been studied before. These include conjugal roles, motherhood, pregnancy, childbirth and childcare.
- It has analysed the contribution of housework to the economy.

Feminism has therefore helped to correct the masculine bias in the previous sociology of the family and to illuminate family life from the perspective of women.

Examiners' notes

This study can be linked to evidence of increasing family diversity (see p 28).

Examiners' notes

Studies of the growth of gay and lesbian families are very useful for answering a wide range of questions about the family, including those on theories of the family, threats to the family, increasing diversity and the direction of social change affecting the family.

Examiners' notes

The highest marks for evaluation tend to be given to those who have a balanced discussion – that is, they look at both the strengths and weaknesses of a perspective, approach or study. This applies to 20-mark essay questions on both the AS and A-level papers.

Introduction to the New Right/neoliberalism

New Right/neoliberal views are associated with the Conservative Party in Britain and others who support right-wing political policies and traditional social values about marriage and family life. The term 'the New Right' was typically applied to the views of the Conservative governments of Margaret Thatcher and John Major from 1979 to 1997, but more recently (for example, during the Conservative governments of David Cameron and Theresa May since 2010) the term 'neoliberalism' has been more widely used.

The New Right/neoliberal perspective strongly supports **free-market** capitalism. It believes that the state should intervene as little as possible in the economy, leaving **private enterprise** to generate wealth. From this viewpoint **competition** benefits consumers and society as a whole by driving down the price of goods while driving up the quality. New Right/neoliberal thinkers see markets as based on choice and believe they encourage individual liberty.

The New Right/neoliberalism and the family

However, New Right/neoliberal theorists do not see choice and liberty as being so important in terms of family life. Instead, they see traditional nuclear families as the cornerstone of stability in society. They favour traditional families for the following reasons:

- They see them as encouraging self-reliance – family members help each other rather than relying on the state.
- This helps to reduce state expenditure on welfare (for example, for lone parents).
- They see families as encouraging shared moral values and believe they are the best way to pass down morality to children.

Unlike functionalists, New Right/neoliberal thinkers do not believe that the family is a stable institution, able to carry out its functions for individuals and society as a whole. Instead they see it as increasingly unstable, leading to an increase in social problems.

The New Right/neoliberalism and policies

When Margaret Thatcher was in power, some policies were introduced to try to support the traditional nuclear family of a married couple and children. For example, in 1988 taxation was changed so that cohabiting couples could no longer claim greater allowances than married couples.

Pamela Abbott and Claire Wallace (1992), however, argue that some of Thatcher's policies allowed or even encouraged people to live outside the traditional nuclear family. For example, divorce laws made it relatively easy for married couples to break up, welfare payments made it easier for mothers to be single parents and illegitimate children were given the same rights as those born to married couples.

Abbott and Wallace believe that Margaret Thatcher's government only introduced a limited range of policies to support nuclear families, and the main emphasis was on saving money.

Under David Cameron from 2010 to 2016 the Conservative/Coalition governments there were some attempts to support traditional family relations (although these were restricted by the Liberal Democrat partners in the coalition government of 2010–15). Cameron gave married couples the right to a tax break if one partner paid a higher rate of tax than the other. This gave some support to families with traditional roles where one partner worked part-time or not at all. However, it was worth a maximum of only £220 a year and also applied to civil partnerships as well as married couples. According to Browne (2012), as with the Thatcher governments, there was more emphasis on saving money.

The decline of the nuclear family?

Some New Right/neoliberal thinkers such as Patricia Morgan (2003) think there is strong evidence of a decline in the traditional nuclear family since the 1970s.

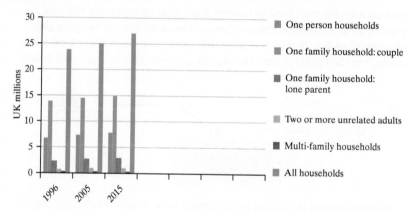

Source: Office for National Statistics, 2015

Notes:
1. One family household: couple and one family household: lone parent can contain dependent and non-dependent children.
2. Households where there is one family and one individual, for example a married couple with their daughter and a lodger or a married couple with one elderly parent are classified as one family household: couple.

Essential notes

Although most of the statistics used by Morgan are accepted, the interpretation of them is not. The changes she describes can be seen as evidence of increasing diversity in families rather than a decline in stability or in the acceptance of family values (see p 36).

Fig 2
Household types in the UK 1996–2015

Criticisms of the New Right/neoliberal perspective

- Advocates of family diversity such as the Rapoports (1989) see increasing diversity as a good thing because it gives people greater freedom to live in the household/family type that best suits them.
- Some sociologists believe that New Right/neoliberal thinkers exaggerate the extent to which family life has changed (see p 36).
- **Feminists** believe that the increase in divorce and single parenthood can be beneficial for women escaping violent, abusive or exploitative relationships with men.
- **Postmodernists** see the declining dominance of nuclear families as part of wider changes in society that are unlikely to be halted by changes in government policies and are in some ways desirable.

Examiners' notes

The critique of this perspective can be developed further by contrasting it with the views of other perspectives.

The relationship between the family and social change

Some theories of the family emphasize the largely unchanging role of the family in society. For example:

- Murdock (see p 4) believed that the family has universal functions and that the nuclear family is typical of all societies.
- **Radical feminists** tend to see families as essentially similar as they are all patriarchal.

Neither of the above approaches acknowledges change in families over time. However, some theorists do acknowledge these changes, including:

- **Liberal feminists** (see p 14) believe that the family is getting less patriarchal.
- **Postmodernists** (see p 22) believe that families are changing as we move into a postmodern era.

Most of these theories tend to believe that a change in society will lead to a change in the family. Parsons (see p 6) believed that a change in the structure of society (from pre-industrial society to industrial society) led to a change in the family (from extended to nuclear). This is illustrated below.

Essential notes

Parsons' concept of structural differentiation looked at on page 7 illustrates how a change in society can lead to a change in the family.

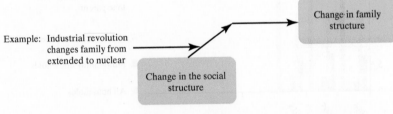

Fig 3
Change from extended to nuclear family

An alternative view is that the family itself can be a cause of change. The structure of the family can shape the direction of change in society. For example, Peter Laslett believed that the dominance of nuclear families helped to cause the Industrial Revolution in some countries.

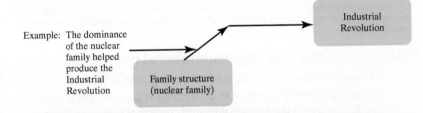

Fig 4
Dominance of the nuclear family

Key study

Talcott Parsons: the family and industrialization

Talcott Parsons believed that the extended family was well-suited to pre-industrial societies because:

- Most people worked in agriculture. All family members worked the land.

- Many children stayed on the family land.

Therefore large families tended to live together across generations.

However, with the development of **industrialization** from the 18th century onwards, extended families were no longer well-suited to the social structure. Industrial employment required a **geographically mobile** workforce who could move to new factories, and this was difficult if there were strong ties of dependency with family members such as grandparents and siblings. Extended families also created status problems (see p 7). The development of industrialism therefore led to a decline in the extended family and its replacement with the nuclear family.

Examiners' notes

Parsons' theory provides a very useful starting point for any discussions of changes in the family in modern Western societies.

Problems with Parsons' theory

- Parsons simply assumed the extended family was the most common family type before the Industrial Revolution.
- Research by Peter Laslett (1972, 1977) found that from 1564 to 1821 only about 10% of households in England contained **kin** beyond the nuclear family.
- Research by Michael Anderson (1971, 1977) focusing on the industrial town of Preston in the mid-19th century found that nearly a quarter of households contained kin other than the nuclear family.
- Research by Michael Young and Peter Wilmot (1973) found that the extended family survived in working-class areas of London into the 1950s.

Essential notes

Research into the development of family types and family networks in the 20th century provides further evidence to contradict Talcott Parsons and to show how changes in society can affect the family (see p 7).

Laslett – an alternative theory

Peter Laslett found that the nuclear family was the norm in north-west parts of Europe before the Industrial Revolution. He argues that family structure was a factor helping to produce the Industrial Revolution rather than being a consequence of it. Industrialization occurred first in Europe because the nuclear family provided the mobile workforce necessary for industry to develop.

The family and social change: conclusion

Although there may be occasions when the structure of the family helps to shape wider changes in society, most sociologists tend to believe that it is changes in society that produce changes in the family. For example:

- The increasing employment of married women outside the home has led to some changes in **conjugal roles** (see p 50).
- Migration and the growth of ethnic minority populations in Britain may have affected the structure of British families (see p 66).

It can be concluded that social structure and family structure are interrelated and affect one another.

The stages of family development

The development of family structures in Britain has been described in a study by Willmott and Young.

Key study

Willmott and Young – The stages of family life

Willmott and Young (1973) claim that the family has been through three stages.

Stage 1: The pre-industrial family is a unit of production with parents and children forming the core.

Stage 2: The early industrial family extended its network to include other kin. There was a strong bond between married daughters and their mothers who often lived close together, even if not under the same roof. This family type continued into the 1950s in working-class areas such as Bethnal Green in London.

Stage 3: In the 1970s the nuclear family became dominant. It was based on a strong conjugal bond between husband and wife, and other relatives outside the nuclear family lost importance. Willmott and Young describe this family as **symmetrical**. By this they mean that the husband and wife have similar roles, both do paid work and both do housework and childcare. It developed because of:

* rising wages and a developing welfare state making nuclear families more self-reliant
* increasing geographical mobility affecting **kinship networks**
* improved entertainment and facilities in the home
* small family size i.e. fewer children per couple.

Families in the 1980s and 1990s

Willmott and Young's research suggests that the extended family will become less and less important as time goes on, but some research contradicts this.

McGlone et al. (1996) argue that **kin** outside the nuclear family are important because they can provide both practical and emotional support. For example, the parents of married children might offer:

* advice
* financial help
* assistance with childcare
* emotional support in times of crisis.

Although kin may live some distance apart, rising living standards, growing car ownership and technological developments make it much easier to keep in touch and to visit one another. McGlone et al. found that contacts remained frequent, with the working class having more contact with kin than the **middle class**.

Essential notes

Some aspects of Willmott and Young's study have been criticized. For example, feminists such as Oakley have questioned the idea of the symmetrical family, pointing out that Willmott and Young found that many men made only a token contribution to housework.

Essential notes

The middle class might see kin less often than the working class, but the contacts can still be important. For example, middle-class parents might be able to offer more financial support than working-class parents.

Research findings on the importance of family life

Research suggests that most people continue to attach a great deal of importance to family life, are family centred and do maintain frequent contact.

- McGlone et al. found that most parents believed they should continue to support their children even after they had left home.
- The British Social Attitudes Survey (2005) shows that the majority of both men (57%) and women (65%) see family members or other relatives weekly or nearly every week. Relatives and friends are about equally important in terms of social contacts, with work colleagues and other acquaintances being much less important. Only a small percentage of men (5%) and women (2%) very rarely or never see other family members.
- Research by Catherine Bonvalet, Celine Clement and Jim Ogg (2015) found that in their sample of 'baby boomers' in Paris and London born between 1945 and 1954, very few had cut ties with their family and most retained strong emotional ties and saw their family quite frequently.

Family structures in contemporary society

A variety of descriptions have been used to characterize family structures in contemporary Britain.

- Peter Willmott (1988) sees the **dispersed extended family** as typical. Most people live in nuclear families but contacts with extended family members who may live some distance apart remain important.
- Julia Brannen (2003) uses the term **beanpole family** to describe families today. She believes there are strong **intergenerational** links between grandparents, children and grandchildren but links with siblings and cousins (**intragenerational** links) are much less important.
- Margaret O'Brien and Deborah Jones (1996) found in research in East London that no one family type is now dominant. Instead there is a **pluralization of lifestyles**. It is therefore pointless to try and find a single family type because family diversity is now the norm (see p 28).

Essential notes

O'Brien and Jones found the strongest and most conventional family structures amongst the Bangladeshi community.

Essential notes

Theories of diversity contradict the claim that a single family type is dominant.

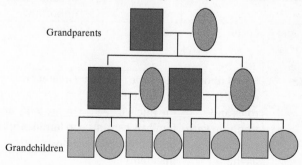

Fig 5
Beanpole family structure

Modernity

Some sociologists divide the development of society into historical time periods. They believe, for example, that society has passed through three stages:

1. pre-modern, pre-industrial society
2. **modern,** industrial society
3. **postmodern, post-industrial** society.

In pre-industrial societies, life was relatively stable and predictable, people acted on the basis of tradition, and roles within society were relatively fixed.

The key change with the development of **modernity** (modern society) is that social life becomes based upon **rationality** rather than tradition and the teachings of religion. That is, instead of acting in ways that religious leaders tell them to, or in the ways they have been brought up to behave, people calculate how they should act to achieve certain goals and this guides their behaviour. As a result, social life is less predictable and increased uncertainty and more rapid change is introduced.

The postmodern era (see p 22) leads to a decline in rationality. More choices are open to individuals and their **identity** becomes less fixed. This results in even more of the uncertainty and change that was typical of the modern era.

Some of the main changes that have been associated with these eras are summarized in the table below.

	Pre-modern	Modern	Postmodern
Basis of economy	Agriculture	Industry	Services/ knowledge economy
Social classes	Landowners/ serfs	Bourgeoisie/ proletariat	Classes lose significance
Main belief system	Religion/ tradition	Science/ rationality	No dominant belief system
Main source of identity	Family	Social class	Diverse and image/ lifestyle based. Ethnicity, sexuality become more important
Geographical basis of social life	Local	National	Global
Family life	Based upon established roles and tradition with marriage as the cornerstone	Marriage remains important and the nuclear family is central, but increasing instability develops	Greater choice and variety develops in sexuality and in families and households

Table 4
Stages in the development of Western societies

20

Other sociologists do not believe that we have yet entered a postmodern era and believe that we still live in modern societies. Their views are examined in this section. According to these sociologists, families have changed as a result of the changes taking place in the modern era (modernity).

Anthony Giddens – relationships in the modern world

Giddens (1992) believes that intimate relationships have changed with modernity.

- In the early period of modernity in the 18th century, marriage became more than an economic arrangement as the idea of romantic love developed. The marriage partner was idealized as someone who would perfect a person's life. Women kept their virginity waiting for the perfect partner.
- In more recent phases of modernity (Giddens calls this **late modernity**), **plastic sexuality** has developed. This means that sex can be for pleasure rather than conceiving children with your perfect marriage partner. Relationships and marriages are no longer seen as necessarily being permanent.
- Marriage is now based on **confluent love** – love that is dependent upon partners benefiting from the relationship. If they are not fulfilled in their relationship, couples no longer stay together out of a sense of duty, so divorce and relationship breakdown become more common.

People in late modernity are involved in a **reflexive project of self** – they constantly think about ways of improving their own life. Tradition and societal **norms** no longer tie couples together as they once did.

Beck and Beck-Gernsheim – individualization

Beck and Beck-Gernsheim (1995) see **individualization** as the main characteristic of modern life. This involves:

- More opportunities for individuals, especially women, and the opportunity for individuals to take more and more decisions about every aspect of their lives.
- Little security or intimacy in the everyday world of work, so people seek emotional security in families.
- No generally accepted formula or recipe about love, relationships or family life, so people have to work out their own solutions. For example, the expectations of the roles of husband and wife are no longer clear-cut.
- Conflict resulting from increased choice and uncertainty and also from the pressures of work, where both men and women are expected to compete to achieve career success.
- Increased uncertainty which leads to chaotic personal relationships and helps to explain high divorce rates.

Essential notes

The idea of late modernity indicates that Giddens believes we have not yet reached a postmodern era but rather that changes have taken place in modernity.

Examiners' notes

In 20-mark questions for both AS and A level, Giddens, Beck and Beck-Gernsheim can be very useful for adding theoretical depth to a range of questions on theory, social changes and the family, the supposed decline of the family and so on. This material is also useful for some 10-mark questions.

Essential notes

Beck sees these changes as part of the development of 'risk society' in which people increasingly face risk and uncertainty from man-made problems rather than from hazards in the natural world.

Introduction

The main features of postmodern society are as follows:

- A rejection of any grand theory which tells people how to live their lives. The postmodernist Jean–François Lyotard (1984) calls this an 'incredulity towards **metanarratives**' – by which he means a lack of faith in any 'big stories' about how society should be run or how people should live. This includes a lack of belief in political ideologies such as Marxism and even a lack of belief in traditional views on marriage and family life.
- Because of this there is increasing diversity, choice and fragmentation in social life. People have the ability to choose from a vast array of identities and lifestyles and do not have to conform to the way previous generations lived.
- Divisions based on social class or traditional **gender roles** become less important while lifestyle choices become much more important.
- The media and the images presented in the media become more influential in a **media-saturated society**.
- Society changes rapidly as new technology is introduced and improved communications lead to a globalization of social life.

Judith Stacey – the postmodern family

The American sociologist Judith Stacey (1996) believes that the postmodern family has developed in the USA. Based on a study of families in Silicon Valley, California, she describes the postmodern family as 'contested, ambivalent, and undecided'. Stacey believes that in the modern era the heterosexual nuclear family was judged to be the norm and the closer a family was to that norm the more it was valued. In the postmodern era she sees families as 'diverse, fluid and unresolved'. In other words they:

- are very varied in the structure and form they take
- are constantly changing
- have no set structure that is regarded as the ideal.

For example, gay and lesbian families have to work out their own set of relationships since they cannot model themselves on the heterosexual nuclear family.

Key study

Judith Stacey – Postmodern families in Silicon Valley

Stacey's ideas are based upon her study of families in Silicon Valley in California, which she sees as a typical post-industrial and postmodern region specializing in the production of silicon chips.

Stacey uses the example of two families/kinship networks to illustrate the nature of postmodern families.

Pam and Dotty

Pam and Dotty were married manual workers at the end of the 1950s and both their husbands worked their way up until they had middle class levels of income. Pam and Dotty did some unskilled manual work to boost family income. Pam and Dotty met in the 1970s when they started courses at a local college where they were exposed to feminist ideas. Both were unhappy with the lack of contribution their husbands made to family life and Dotty was physically abused by her husband.

Pam got divorced and started a degree, later marrying a man with whom she had a more equal relationship. She also befriended her first husband's live-in lover to form an unusual extended kinship network.

Dotty split up with her husband as well, but eventually took him back after he had had a serious heart attack and was no longer physically able to abuse her. Her husband now had to do most of the housework and Dotty started campaigning for the rights of battered women. After her husband and two of her adult children died, Dotty formed a new household consisting of her, one of her surviving daughters who was a single mother, and four grandchildren.

Pam and Dotty's families demonstrate the fluid and constantly changing family and household structures in Silicon Valley that are typical of postmodernity.

Essential notes

Whatever the limitations of this particular study, there is no doubt that family life is becoming more varied.

Evaluation of postmodern theories of the family

Stacey's study can be criticized for:

- research based on a very small sample of families
- exaggerating the degree of fluidity and uncertainty in family life by picking untypical examples
- underestimating the continuing appeal of heterosexual nuclear families.

However, in more recent research in her book *Unhitched* Stacey provides more examples from a range of countries including South Africa and China suggesting that love, marriage and child-rearing are no longer necessary closely linked and family diversity is a world-wide phenomenon.

Postmodern perspectives do provide an explanation for increasing diversity of family types (see pp 28–37) although the explanations are quite generalized.

Introduction

The family has sometimes been regarded as a private sphere in which the state should not interfere. However, there is no doubt that in Britain a number of state policies have a direct and indirect impact upon family and that the government sometimes deliberately tries to intervene in aspects of family life. For example, the state can affect family life through:

- Education policies such as the provision of nursery education and compulsory schooling.
- Taxation policies such as the way the incomes of husbands and wives are taxed.
- Legal changes such as changes in divorce law or child protection legislation.
- Housing policy such as the suitability and location of social housing.
- Health and welfare policies, such as 'care in the community', which affects the responsibility of families for relatives.

Country	Policy	Outcome of policy
Communist Soviet Union	The state tried to undermine the family in line with the Marxist view that families would not be necessary in communist societies as they only existed to bolster the power of the ruling class in capitalism. In the 1920s legislation encouraged equality between the sexes and liberalized divorce and abortion laws.	By the 1930s the state was encouraging family life and the role of women in giving birth in order to increase the size of the population.
Kibbutz in Israel	In kibbutzim, children were raised separately from their parents with full-time carers looking after them. Parents lived close by and visited them daily.	Policy was gradually abandoned as conventional family units were preferred by most people.
Communist China	Since 1980, couples who have more than one child have been fined and some parents have been fired from their jobs. Many women have been forced into having abortions. In the countryside parents are allowed to have a second child if the first is a girl but this is not allowed in the cities.	Policy has resulted in a rapidly ageing population and disproportionate number of males (as female foetuses are more likely to be aborted), but has yet to be lifted.

Table 5
Family policies in different societies

Sociological and political perspectives on the family

The New Right/neoliberalism

As discussed on page 14, the New Right/neoliberals are strongly in favour of conventional nuclear families with married heterosexual couples living with their children. They see this family structure as providing stability as well as being independent and self-reliant. If family members care for each other (for example, families taking care of elderly relatives), this reduces state expenditure and allows taxes to be kept low which benefits private enterprise. They also believe that nuclear families pass on a work ethic to their children and this benefits free-market economies.

Charles Murray (1984) argues that an **underclass** has been created through over-generous welfare payments, especially to single parents. Single parenthood is harmful to society because it encourages irresponsible behaviour amongst children who copy the parents. Sons of single mothers miss an adult male role model of a hard-working and responsible father taking care of his family. Daughters of single mothers may follow in the mother's footsteps by having children outside of stable relationships, often while they are young, and then relying upon state benefits to support them.

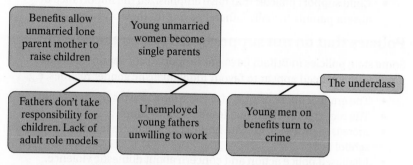

Fig 6
The causes of the underclass

The New Right/neoliberalism influenced the policies of Conservative governments between 1979 and 1997, particularly in the period when Margaret Thatcher was in power. To a lesser extent they also influenced the Coalition and Conservative governments of David Cameron and Theresa May from 2010 onwards.

Feminist views

As discussed on page 10, feminists are critical of the nuclear family, arguing that it is usually patriarchal and biased in favour of men. Feminists believe that social policies generally act to maintain the power of men in families and do little to control men who are violent or abusive to their partners or children. Feminists therefore tend to favour policies which give more choice to women, including liberal divorce laws and tax and benefits policies which make women independent of their male partners.

> **Examiners' notes**
>
> It is useful to refer to different types of gender regime to add theoretical substance to the content of answers.

Key study

Eileen Drew – Gender regimes

An example of feminist research on social policy and family is provided by Eileen Drew (1995), who argues that the policies of different governments follow different **gender regimes** – sets of policies which make different assumptions about family life. There are two main types of gender regime:

- **Familistic gender regimes** favour and support traditional nuclear families in which husbands are expected to be the main breadwinner while wives are expected to concentrate on domestic responsibilities.
- **Individualistic gender regimes** have more egalitarian policies, believing that assumptions should not be made about the roles of husbands and wives and they should be treated equally. This type of gender regime is more tolerant of the choices that individuals make and is more accepting of diversity in family life.

Drew argues that many countries are moving towards a more individualistic gender regime. Whether this is the case in Britain is examined below.

Policies that support conventional families

A number of policies that support conventional families (or familistic gender regimes) have been identified by sociologists. These include:

- The assumption that child benefit should be paid to mothers.
- School hours that assume one parent will be at home in the afternoon making it difficult for **dual-earner families**.

Essential notes

The Child Support Agency
was set up in 2003 to pursue
maintenance payments
and was replaced in 2008
by the Child Maintenance
and Support Commission.
This prevents single-parent
families having to be self-
sufficient, although its
principal aim may be to save
the state money.

Essential notes

The Child Support Agency
was set up in 2003 to pursue
maintenance payments
and was replaced in 2008
by the Child Maintenance
and Support Commission.
This prevents single-parent
families having to be self-
sufficient, although its
principal aim may be to save
the state money.

Examiners' notes

Answers should balance
evidence which suggests that
conventional families are
supported by policies with
evidence that they are not,
before reaching a conclusion
about the overall effect.

Essential notes

Whatever the philosophy
underlying the policies of
different parties, in the end
most tend to only intervene
directly in family life to a
limited extent.

- Limited state provision of care for the elderly and the
  encouragement of relatives (usually daughters) to provide care.
- According to Fox Harding (1996), housing policies that assume
  nuclear families should get priority over lone parent families.
- Child support policies that have emphasized the importance of
  absent parents (usually fathers) paying for their offspring.

Policies that do not support conventional families

Some state policies in Britain have not supported conventional nuclear
families and instead appear to favour individualistic gender regimes, e.g:

- The gradual liberalization of divorce laws (see p 42).
- The recognition of gay and lesbian relationships.
- Increased provision of state funding for childcare for children under
  school age.
- Increased police action and concern about domestic violence,
  particularly that committed by men against women.

Social policies and the family

Supporting conventional families	Undermining conventional families
• Education hours • Child benefit • Family tax credit • Family-sized social housing • Child support policies for fathers • Expectation of family care for elderly	• Benefits for lone parents • Legalization of civil partnerships for gay/lesbian couples and of same-sex marriage • Liberal divorce law • State help with childcare for under-fives • Prosecution of violent husbands

Policies and political parties

Sociologists have examined the extent to which recent British governments
have favoured the view that the conventional, single-earner nuclear family
is the ideal.

New Right/neoliberal governments, 1979 to 1997

According to Pamela Abbott and Claire Wallace (1992), the governments
of Margaret Thatcher and John Major followed some policies supporting
traditional families. For example:

- They changed taxation policies so that cohabiting couples could no
  longer claim more in tax allowances than married couples.

However:

- They did not introduce tax or benefits policies to encourage mothers
  to stay at home.
- They made divorce easier to obtain in 1984.
- They gave illegitimate children the same rights as those born within
  marriage.

Abbott and Wallace conclude that in reality the New Right/neoliberal had a more balanced approach to families than their ideology would suggest.

New Labour, 1997 to 2010

The New Labour party followed the New Right/neoliberal in arguing that the traditional family was a desirable institution. However:

- New Labour was more willing to accept that family diversity was the norm and that policies should reflect this.
- They allowed civil partnerships for gay and lesbian couples and also allowed these couples the right to be able to apply to adopt children.

This suggests that New Labour adopted a more individualistic gender regime than the previous Conservative government.

Some New Labour policies supported nuclear families:

- They gave employees the right to time off work for family reasons.
- They introduced a Working Families Tax Credit .

Jennifer Somerville (2000) claims that Tony Blair's government idealized family life as a 'working example of mutual interdependence, care and responsibility' and increased expectations about parental responsibility, even though it recognized diversity.

Coalition and conservative governments from 2010

In 2010 David Cameron became Prime Minister in a coalition government between Conservatives and Liberal Democrats. The Conservatives gained power on their own in the 2015 general election under David Cameron. He was replaced by Theresa May in 2016 following the Brexit vote.

Cameron introduced a small tax break for married couples, suggesting support for conventional nuclear families. However, at the party conference in 2010, it was announced that Child Benefit would be stopped for families with a higher rate taxpayer.

Research by James Browne (2012) into tax and benefits policies announced by 2012 found that in reality families with children in reliant on benefits would be hardest hit of all households by the changes.

Following the 2011 riots Cameron tried to focus policy on trying to help 'troubled families' by which he meant lone parent families without a father at home, echoing to some extent Charles Murray's ideas on the 'underclass' (see pp 24-25). However, Haralambos and Holborn (2013) note that tax and benefits changes actually created disincentives for couples with children who claimed benefits to continue to live together.

Conclusion

Once in power all recent governments have had to acknowledge the reality of increasing family diversity and none have succeeded in reversing a move away from traditional gender roles in conventional nuclear families.

Essential notes

John Major's government introduced a 'back to basics' campaign extolling the virtues of conventional morality and family life, but it was undermined when the infidelity of some cabinet ministers was exposed.

Essential notes

The Working Families Tax Credit helped with the finances of families.

Essential notes

Stopping Child Benefits for families with a higher rate tax payer disadvantages affluent families with a single earner and a stay-at-home mother – dual-earner families could earn much more than single-earner families without losing the benefit.

What is family diversity?

A good deal of historical research on the family has sought to identify the typical family type in different eras. For example, research has examined whether the nuclear family is the typical or dominant type in industrial societies. The idea of family diversity suggests that in any one era, no particular type of family is dominant or can be considered the norm.

Some historians such as Michael Anderson (1980) have argued that there has always been diversity in family types, but most sociologists of the family before the 1980s assumed that family diversity was not the norm. More recently some sociologists have continued to argue that a single family type is dominant. For example, Peter Willmott (1988) claims that the dispersed extended family is the norm and Julia Brannen (2003) believes that the beanpole family is now typical in Britain (see p 19).

The cereal packet image of the family

The idea that a single family type is dominant is also found in the media. According to Ann Oakley (1982), marketing and advertising often tries to sell products to what it sees as a typical family. Oakley believes that the image of the typical family presented, for example, in advertising for breakfast cereals, portrays the conventional family as 'nuclear families composed of legally married couples, voluntarily choosing the parenthood of one or more (but not too many) children'. Leach (1967) calls this the **cereal packet image of the family**.

The portrayal of the cereal packet image of the family has been attacked by the American feminist Barrie Thorne (1992). Thorne believes that gender, generation, race and class result in widely varying experiences of family life, many of which diverge from the nuclear family with the male **breadwinner** and female housewife.

Oakley, Leach and Thorne all see this stereotype of the nuclear family as highly misleading, and the idea that diversity or variation in families is normal has been developed by other sociologists.

Family diversity in Britain

Robert and Rhona Rapoport (1982) were the first British sociologists to point out that nuclear family households have become a minority in Britain. Since they first wrote about diversity, nuclear families have continued to become a smaller proportion of all households in Great Britain.

In table 7 the categories 'One family household with 1–2, or 3 or more dependent children' represent the nuclear family. In 1971 35% of households were of this type but by 2010 the figure had decreased to 21%. The table shows that there have been increases in the percentage of households consisting of one person under or over state pension age, a couple, and lone parents with dependent or non-dependent children.

Examiners' notes

It is useful to discuss diversity when answering any questions about the structure of the family today because diversification is an essential part of all recent trends in family life.

Examiners' notes

Note that the ideas of both Oakley and Thorne can also be used to answer questions about the contribution of feminists to an understanding of the family.

Household types increasing 1971–2008	One person households under pension age.
	One person households over pension age.
	Couple only households.
	Lone parent households with dependent children.
	Lone parent households with non-dependent children.
Household types decreasing 1971–2008	One family households with 1–2 dependent children.
	One family households with three or more dependent children.
	One family households with non-dependent children.
	Households with two or more unrelated adults.

Examiners' notes

To give a rounded answer to questions about family diversity you will also need to look at page 31, which includes some alternative interpretations of the trends shown in these statistics. Not everybody agrees that the figures show a serious decline in nuclear families.

Table 6
Growing and declining household types, 1961–2010

Households: by type of household and family						
Great Britain			**Percentages**			
	1961	1971	1981	1991	2001	2010
One person households	12	18	22	27	29	29
One family households						
Couple						
No children	26	27	26	28	29	28
1–2 dependent children	30	26	25	20	19	18
3 or more dependent children	8	9	6	5	4	3
Non-dependent children only	10	8	8	8	6	6
Lone parent						
Dependent children	2	3	5	6	7	7
Non-dependent children only	4	4	4	4	3	3
Two or more unrelated adults	5	4	5	3	3	3
Multi-family households	3	1	1	1	1	1
All households						
(=100%) (millions)	16.3	18.6	20.2	22.4	23.9	25.3

Table 7
Data on households in the UK, 1961–2010
Source: Social Trends (2011)

These changes represent an increase in the diversity of family structures and in the proportion of households with a structure other than that of the nuclear family.

Types of diversity

The Rapoports (1982) identify five main types of diversity:

1. **Organizational diversity**. This involves variations in family structure, household type, kinship network and the **division of labour** within the home. Examples include **lone-parent families**, dual-earner families, **cohabiting** couples and **reconstituted families** (families formed out of the fragments of previous families after a divorce). Reconstituted families can include stepchildren, half brothers and sisters and so on.
2. Cultural diversity. This refers to differences in lifestyles between families of different ethnic, national or religious backgrounds; for example, differences between British Asian and white British families, British and Polish families, Catholic and Protestant families.
3. Class diversity. There are also differences in families of upper-class, middle-class and working-class origin. These might impact on relationships between adults and the way children are socialized.
4. Stage in the **life-cycle**. For example, there are differences between newly married couples without children, couples with dependent children and families with non-dependent children.
5. Cohort. A cohort is a group of people born over the same period of time (e.g. the baby boomer generation born in the period 1946 to 1964). This generation is sometimes seen as having a different pattern of family life than their parents' generation; for example, having more dual-earner families.

One type of family diversity which was not noted by the Rapoports was sexual diversity. This is discussed on the following page.

Reasons for diversification

Graham Allan and Graham Crow (2001) believe that diversification has continued. There is no longer a fixed set of stages in the life-cycle and each family follows a more unpredictable course, complicated by cohabitation, divorce, remarriage, and so on. This reflects greater individual choice and 'the increasing separation of sex, marriage and parenthood'.

They give the following reasons for increasing diversity:

- A rising divorce rate caused by factors such as divorce law changes, rising social acceptance of divorce and more independence for women.
- An increase in lone parent households partly resulting from increasing divorce, also from greater acceptance of births outside marriage.
- Cohabitation has become increasingly acceptable, partly as a result of the decline in the influence of religion (secularization).
- Declining marriage rates, as people marry later and an increasing minority choose not to marry at all.
- The rise in the number of **stepfamilies** as a result of increases in divorce.

Rates of cohabitation have increased, with each cohort adding to family diversity. The number of people marrying is falling but more than a quarter of marriages are remarriages, leading to the formation of more reconstituted families.

New types of diversity

Over recent decades, new types of diversity in addition to those identified by the Rapoports have developed as a result of liberalization in attitudes to sexuality and the introduction of **new reproductive technologies**. The Civil Partnerships Act of 2004 recognized and legitimized gay and lesbian relationships in the UK, and in 2014 it became possible for same-sex couples to get married on the same basis as heterosexual couples.

- Weeks, Heaphey and Donovan (1999) see the increase in openly gay and lesbian households and families as contributing to the increase in diversity. They believe that gay men and lesbians often see their households and even their friendship networks as being chosen families. On the basis of this they argue that an important social change is taking place in which whom we see to be part of our family is more important than ties of blood or marriage. **Friendship networks** can now function as if they were families. This is part of a general move towards a greater emphasis on individual choice rather than the duties and obligations of family life.
- Roseneil (2005) links the development of chosen families to the breakdown of the **heteronorm** – the belief that all intimate relationships should be based on heterosexuality. TV programmes such as *Friends* and *Will and Grace* highlight the possibility that there are alternative networks to traditional families.

New reproductive technologies

New reproductive technologies date from 1978 when the first 'test-tube baby', Louise Brown, was born through in-vitro fertilization.

Surrogate motherhood, where one woman carries a foetus produced by the egg of another woman, is now possible. This raises questions about who the parents of the child are since the birth parents and the genetic parents are different. It adds to the complexity of possible family types and has even led to a grandmother giving birth to her own grandchild.

Examiners' notes

The idea of chosen families is extremely useful in answering a wide range of questions. It challenges conventional definitions of the family since it means that families are no longer based on kinship or marriage and it can therefore be used to question most of the theories of the family. It does, however, fit with the postmodern view of the family which sees traditional assumptions about the family as no longer being accepted.

The growth of single parenthood

Lone parenthood can come about through a number of different routes. People who are married can become lone parents through divorce, **separation** or the death of a spouse. Similarly, cohabiting parents who are not married and have children can split up or one of them die. It can also result from births to women who do not live with the father of the child.

As table 8 shows, the percentage of households with children that are headed by lone parents has increased steadily, rising from 8% in 1971 to 22% in 2011. Only a small minority are lone fathers (1% in 1971 and 2% in 2011). It is significant that the percentage of households with children headed by widows has actually gone down whereas the percentage that are single has increased five-fold, the percentage divorced has gone up 250% and the percentage that is separated has doubled.

	1971 (%)	1991 (%)	2011 (%)
Married/cohabiting couple	92	81	78
Lone mother	7	18	20
Single	2	6	10
Widowed	2	1	1
Divorced	2	6	5
Separated	2	4	4
Lone fathers	1	1	2
All lone parents	8	19	22

Table 8
Family type and marital status of lone parents 1971–2011
Source: based on figures from Social Trends (2011)

Demographic causes of lone parenthood

Allan and Crow (2001) explain the increase in lone parenthood in terms of two factors:

- an increase in **marital breakdown** (particularly divorce)
- a rise in births to unmarried mothers.

They suggest that both these trends can be explained in terms of an increasing acceptance of diversity and choice in family life. (See pp 38–39 for explanations of rising divorce).

David Morgan (1994) sees changing relationships between men and women as important, with greater equality between the sexes making it more feasible for women to bring up children on their own. In addition, more employment opportunities for women encourage them to have a life in which they are not dependent upon a male partner.

Changing attitudes and lone parenthood

Evidence from the British Social Attitudes Survey (2014) shows that there have been significant changes in attitudes. In 1989, 70% of respondents said that couples who wanted children should marry but in 2012 just 42% thought this.

Similarly, sex before marriage has become much more widely accepted, helping to explain the increase in single lone parents. In 1983, 42% said this was 'Not wrong at all', but by 2012 this had increased to 65%. The 2012 survey also found that younger generations had more liberal attitudes towards sex and marriage than older generations. David Morgan (1994) notes that much less stigma is now attached to **illegitimacy**. However, research by Burghes and Brown (1995) suggests that most lone parents do not regard the situation as ideal and the British Social Attitudes Survey found there is still disapproval of teenage pregnancies. (In 2006 only 42% agreed that one parent can bring up a child as well as two parents).

Dependency culture

According to Charles Murray (1999) the increase in lone parenthood is a result of an over-generous welfare system which makes it possible for lone parents to live on benefits with housing provided by the state. Murray sees lone parents as part of a welfare-dependent underclass.

Murray's views have been strongly criticized for being based on limited research.

Allan and Crow (2001) point out that most lone mothers find a new partner within a few years and do not rely on benefits throughout an offspring's childhood. This view is supported by research by the Department for Work and Pensions (2004).

The effects of lone parenthood

Some research suggests that lone parenthood can lead to a range of negative consequences, particularly for the children. These include:

- a greater chance of living in **poverty**
- children doing less well in education
- children being more likely to become delinquent or to use drugs.

However, more sophisticated research suggests that any negative effects are more the result of low income than the lack of two parents. Research in 2005 by Nick Spencer found that material deprivation was very largely responsible for the reduced life chances of the children of lone parents rather than the type of family they grew up in. E.E. Cashmore (1985) points out that having one parent may be better for children than having two parents if the absent parent is abusive or violent.

Examiners' notes

Charles Murray is associated with the theory of the New Right/neoliberals – his ideas are dealt with on page 25. This perspective can be criticized using other theories, particularly feminism and postmodernism. Incorporating criticisms from competing theoretical perspectives helps to get you into the top mark band.

Essential notes

Many studies which claim there are negative effects of lone parenthood for children can be criticized on methodological grounds. Most use small samples and fail to control for the effects of low income on outcomes for children. More sophisticated research does control for the effects of low income/poverty and this tends to find less strong evidence of negative consequences.

Ethnicity and diversity

- Ethnic groups are groups within a population regarded by themselves or others as culturally distinctive; they usually see themselves as having a common origin. Ethnicity may be linked to religion, nationality and other aspects of culture such as language and lifestyle.
- Largely as a result of **migration**, Britain has a number of distinctive ethnic groups. The largest minority ethnic groups in Britain are those of South Asian or African Caribbean origin. The Irish and Chinese can also be regarded as minority ethnic groups. Recent migration from Eastern Europe has increased the size of white minority ethnic groups in the UK.
- Minority ethnic groups can be seen as adding to the diversity of family types in Britain to the extent that they have distinctive family patterns or lifestyles. If their family life has become very similar to that of the white British majority then minority ethnic groups may not contribute to the diversity.

The extent of ethnic diversity

The statistics available on families and ethnic diversity suggest significant differences in the types of family and household structure typical of different ethnic groups.

Table 9, based on the Labour Force Survey, shows that:

- Black Caribbean households are four times more likely to consist of a lone parent with dependent children than 'White Other' and Indian households.
- Chinese households have an exceptionally high percentage of single people but a very low percentage of lone parents.
- British Asian households have the highest percentages of couples with dependent children.
- White households have the highest percentage of households without dependent children.

Other data from the same source shows that average family size is highest for Pakistanis and Bangladeshis, and lowest for the Chinese.

The 2011 Census also found significant differences between ethnic groups and their families and households. For example, 10.3% of White British, but just 2.5% of Bangladeshi, households were headed by an unmarried, cohabiting couple.

The 2001 census found that 71% of Black Caribbean adults were single (never married) compared to 39% of White British adults, but just 8% of Pakistanis and 5% of Bangladeshis.

Examiners' notes

Be prepared to answer individual questions on ethnicity and family life but also to integrate material on this topic into general questions about family diversity.

Ethnic group	Family type (%)			
	Single person	Couple no dependent children	Couple with dependent children	Lone parent with dependent children
White British	36	35	20	9
White Other	45	30	18	7
Indian	30	30	33	7
Pakistani	24	19	45	11
Bangladeshi	20	14	52	14
Black Caribbean	41	14	16	28
Chinese	56	21	17	6

Table 9
Family types in England and Wales by ethnic group, 2009

Studies of Asian families

Research by Bhatti (1999) using in-depth interviews of Asian families in southern England found a strong emphasis on family loyalty and on trying to maintain traditional family practices. Izzat, the principle of family honour, was taken very seriously and mothers saw their family roles as the most important duty in life. Fathers usually took on the traditional breadwinner role. This evidence suggests that Asian families add to diversity by maintaining traditional, nuclear families but with very strong extended kinship networks and a strong sense of mutual obligation.

However, there was some evidence that life in Britain has begun to erode the distinctiveness of Asian families, with increasing numbers of clashes between younger and older generations. In some families children rebelled against traditional values, for example by seeking to marry outside their own community against parental wishes.

A study of British Asians living in Brick Lane – the heart of the Bangladeshi community in Britain – by the Policy Studies Institute (1997) found that British South Asians were more likely to marry and to marry earlier than white counterparts and that rates of divorce and lone parenthood were low, although they were beginning to increase.

Studies of African Caribbean families

The Policy Studies Institute (1997) found that British African Caribbean households had fewer long-term partnerships than other groups, were more likely to have children outside marriage and had above average rates of divorce and separation.

Research by Mary Chamberlain (1999) has found that brothers, sisters, uncles and aunts play a more important role in African Caribbean families than in white British families. Siblings often play a significant part in bringing up younger brothers and sisters and women are quite likely to assist sisters in bringing up children.

Tracey Reynolds (2002) argues that despite the large number of female-headed households amongst Black-Caribbean families in Britain, in reality diversity is the main characteristic of family life in this group. As well as conventional nuclear families and **female-headed families**, **visiting relationships** are also common where the female head of household has a male partner who visits them frequently but does not live under the same roof.

Conclusion

The evidence suggests that ethnic minorities do continue to add to the diversity of family life, though there has been some convergence with the family life of white British families. Vanessa May (2015) argues that the family practices of minority ethnic groups in Britain are changing so that traditional views on family and marriage are influential but they adapt to British circumstances. For example, amongst British Pakistanis sons are now more likely to have relationships before marriage and great importance is now attached to girls' education partly because the possibility of divorce is accepted.

Examiners' notes

You can get into a higher mark band by showing that you are aware of differences between specific ethnic groups. For example, amongst South Asians there are significant differences, with considerably higher rates of one person households amongst Indians (30%) than Bangladeshis (20%).

Examiners' notes

Markers will be looking to see if you have compared patterns of family life in ethnic minorities with majority, white British, patterns and if you have demonstrated an awareness of changes over time. Use the studies to indicate whether the family life of different ethnic groups is becoming more similar over time.

Essential notes

Some sociologists have claimed that there is a distinctive family type among the black population of the Caribbean and the Americas dominated by mothers who are lone parents but get support from other female relatives. Chamberlain's study provides some evidence that this family type has been imported to Britain.

The implications of family diversity

Some researchers see increasing diversity as not only part of a decline of the nuclear family but also as undermining this institution as a model of a conventional family. The following key study backs up this view.

> ### Key study
>
> #### Dench, Gavron and Young – Bethnal Green revisited
>
> Dench, Gavron and Young (2006) carried out a study in Bethnal Green in the 1990s to follow up Young and Willmott's study of the area from the 1950s (see p 18). They found that earlier family patterns where working-class residents lived in nuclear families with strong kinship links had largely disappeared. They have been replaced by a new **individualism** in which **cohabitation**, divorce, separation and lone parenthood were all more common. Only the local Bangladeshi population had a dominant pattern of conventional family life based upon marriage and the male breadwinner.

Such research has led commentators such as Brenda Almond (2006) to claim that the family is fragmenting (breaking into pieces) and is more concerned with the needs of adult members than creating a stable unit in which children can be raised.

Robert Chester – the neo-conventional family

The widespread view that the nuclear family is threatened by diversity and is breaking up or even disappearing has been challenged by Robert Chester (1985). He found that the following main features of family life have remained fairly stable since the Second World War:

- Most people still get married.
- Most children are reared by their natural parents.
- Most people live in a household headed by a married couple.
- Most people stay married.

Although the situation has changed since Chester was writing, most of the above is still true. (Although the proportion of marriages ending in divorce is now approaching 50%.)

Chester argues that the statistics used to support the idea of increasing diversity can be misleading. They are usually based upon the proportion of households of different types and not the proportion of people living in different types of household. This makes a significant difference because nuclear family households tend to be larger than other households since by definition they contain at least two adults and one child. Table 10 shows the percentage of the adult population living in different household types, as well as the percentage of all households of different types.

Great Britain						
	1971	1981	1991	2001	2008	2010
One person households	6%	8%	11%	12%	12%	12%
One family households						
Couple:						
No children	19%	20%	23%	25%	25%	25%
Dependent children	52%	47%	41%	38%	36%	36%
Non-dependent children only	10%	10%	11%	9%	9%	9%
Lone parent	4%	6%	10%	11%	11%	9%
Other households	9%	9%	4%	5%	6%	9%

Table 10
Adults in UK households: by type of household and family

The table shows that in 2010, 70% of people were still living in households headed by a couple. This represented a fall from 81% in 1971 but was still a large majority of the population.

Not all of these families were nuclear families in the sense of including both parents and dependent children but, as Chester points out, couples without dependent children often go on to have children later. Furthermore some one-person households consist of widows and widowers who were once married but whose children have now grown up. Chester concludes that most people still live in nuclear families for much of their lives.

Chester believes that one major change has taken place in the life of nuclear families, a change in the roles of husband and wife. He accepts that, increasingly, married women are employed outside the home and he calls this type of family, in which both parents have paid employment, the **neo-conventional family**.

Conclusion

Elizabeth Silva and Carol Smart (1999) agree with Chester that cohabiting or married couples, many of whom have children or go on to have children, remain very important in contemporary family life.

Jennifer Somerville (2000) agrees the decline in traditional families can be exaggerated but also emphasizes that there are important changes taking place. These include:

- Sex outside marriage becoming common.
- More couples who choose not to have children.
- Increasing numbers of lone parents.
- Greater diversity as a result of variations in the family life of different ethnic groups.

On the other hand, Deborah Chambers (2012) accepts that the nuclear family is an 'icon of tradition and stability, often still perceived as an antidote to today's social problems', but she sees it as 'just one of many diverse living arrangements'.

Essential notes

These views offer some support to those who have tried to identify a single dominant family type in Britain today, such as Julia Brannen, who used the concept of the beanpole family (see p 19). Silva, Smart and Somerville recognize the existence of diversity more than Brannen.

Marriage under threat

Some commentators such as Patricia Morgan (2003) believe that the institution of marriage is under threat from a range of factors. These include:

- Falling marriage rates and people marrying at a later age.
- The growth and increasing acceptance of alternatives to marriage including cohabitation and staying single.
- An increase in **single-person households.**
- Declining **fertility** and **birth rates** even to those who are married.
- Rising divorce rates (examined on pp 40–43).

Marriage rates

Fig 7 shows trends in marriage rates in England and Wales since 1833 and shows that there has been a long-term decline in rates since the early 1970s. In 2013 the marriage rates (marriages per 1,000 unmarried men/women) was 22.5 for men and 20.4 for women (ONS, 2016). There had been small rises from 2009-2012 but the 2013 figures were the lowest on record and they were a fraction of the 1972 figures when the rates were 78.4 for men and 60.5 for women. Just 240,854 marriages took place in 2013.

One reason for the decline in marriage rates may be a delay in the timing of marriage, with both men and women tending to delay marriages until later in life. In 1973 the average age at marriage was 28.8 for men and 26.1 for women but by 2013 these figures had climbed to 36.7 for men and 34.3 for women. These figures include all marriages, including remarriages, but the same trend is evident for first marriages. Average age at first marriage was 32.5 for men and 30.6 years for women; an increase of almost 8 years for both sexes when compared with 1973.

However, since first marriage rates are declining in all age groups it is not just a question of delaying marriage; each successive generation is less likely to get married. Research by Ben Wilson and Steve Smallwood (2007) shows that rates of marriage in England and Wales have fallen for the cohorts of women born in each year between 1974 and 1986.

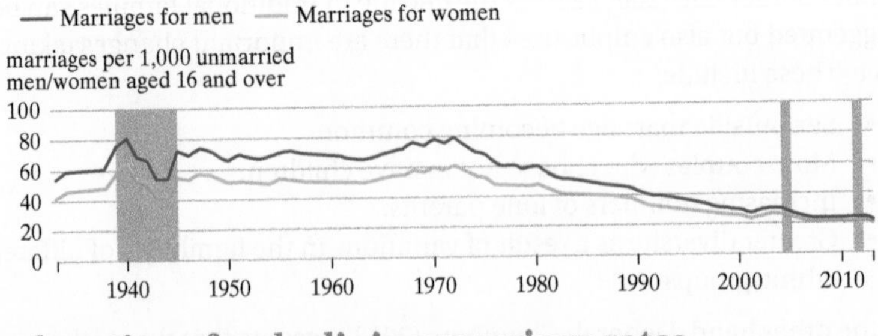

Essential notes

The marriage rate is the number of people per 1000 of the single population getting married each year.

Examiners' notes

You can use data on the changes in marriage rates to answer questions which ask you to discuss whether the family is in decline. Try to remember some simple statistics which will give you solid support for the points you make.

— Marriages for men — Marriages for women

marriages per 1,000 unmarried men/women aged 16 and over

Fig 7
Marriage rates in England and Wales 1933–2013

Explanations for declining marriage rates

Declining marriage rates may be caused by several factors which have made marriage less popular. These include:

- Changing social attitudes which see marriage as less socially desirable than in the past and living outside marriage as more acceptable.

- A decline in religious belief (**secularization**) which weakens commitment to marriage as an institution.
- An increase in cohabitation (see below).
- A greater emphasis on individualism (see p 21 and p 26).

However, declining marriage does not necessarily indicate a decline in commitment to long-term relationships; for example:

- Civil partnerships among gay and lesbian couples have numbered over 60,000 and couples have started to take advantage of the opportunity for same-sex marriages since they were made available in 2014.
- Wilson and Smallwood (2007) point out that marriage rates do not include people married abroad and there is an increasing trend for British couples to travel outside the country to marry.

Cohabitation

Cohabitation has increased rapidly. According to the General Household Survey, in 1979 in Great Britain less than 3% of females were cohabiting but by 2005 this had risen to more than 12%.

In 2004/5, 29% of cohabiting women were divorced, 27% single, 23% separated and 6% widowed.

By 2004/5, around 80% of couples getting married cohabited before their marriage.

Patricia Morgan (2003) sees rising cohabitation as part of a trend in which marriage is going out of fashion. Rather than being a prelude to marriage, Morgan believes that it represents an increase in the number of sexual partners and the frequency of partner change. She notes that cohabiting couples tend to stay together for a shorter time than married couples.

Joan Chandler (1993) disagrees, seeing cohabitation as a relatively stable, long-term alternative to marriage.

The British Social Attitudes Survey (2001) has found evidence of increasing acceptance of cohabitation outside marriage, with younger age groups being more likely to find it acceptable than older age groups. However, these surveys have found that there continues to be strong support for long-term, heterosexual relationships. On average, cohabitants in the survey had lived together for 6½ years. Similarly, research by Beaujouan and Bhrolchain (2011) found that over 60% of cohabitants were still together after 10 years.

However, an alternative trend is for couples, even in stable relationships not to live together. Sasha Roseneil (2015) and others refer to this as **'living apart together'** and Roseneil argues that close relationships which have many of the characteristics of marriage can be sustained without living under the same roof.

Examiners' notes

To get in the top mark band for essay questions, answers may well require some theoretical content, so make reference to theories of modernity and postmodernity if appropriate.

Examiners' notes

You can always get extra marks for making methodological points, and this point raised by Wilson and Smallwood can be used to question the validity of statistics on marriage rates.

Essential notes

Morgan supports New Right/ neoliberal theories (see p 14) so she argues that these changes are part of a pattern of moral decline. She would prefer to see a return to longer relationships, preferably within marriage. Supporters of diversity, though, see these changes as a welcome increase in individual choice.

Types of marital breakdown

Marital breakdown involves the failure or ending of a marriage. This can be divided into three main categories:

1. Divorce, the legal ending of a marriage.
2. Separation, the physical separation of spouses so that they live apart.
3. **'Empty-shell marriages'**, in which husbands and wives continue to live together and remain legally married, but their relationship has broken down.

Trends in divorce

Long-term, the divorce rate (the number of people divorcing per thousand of the married population) has risen dramatically. In 1911 there were just 859 petitions for divorce in England and Wales but in 2014 there were more than 111,000 divorces.

More recently there has been some decline in divorce, with the rate in 2013 down more than 25% on the peak in 2003.

Fig 8
Marriages and divorces in England Wales 1933–2013

Patterns of divorce

The Office for National Statistics figures for England and Wales show that in 2013:

-   A fifth of those married in 1968 (20%) had divorced within 15 years, but nearly a third of those married in 1998 (32%) had divorced within 15 years.
-   Those between 40 and 44 had the highest divorce rate and the mean age at divorce was 45 in 2013.
-   The divorce rate in 2013 was 9.8 per thousand for both men and women, so just under 1 in a hundred married people divorced each year. This was down from a divorce rate of over 13 in 2003.
-   48% of divorcing couples in 2013 had at least one child under 16.
-   Around two-thirds of divorce decrees granted to just one partner are given to women, and around a third to men.
-   Dissolutions of same-sex civil partnerships are increasing but partly because there are more couples who can split up.

Separation statistics

There are no reliable figures for separation. However, the 2001 census found that around 2% of adults are separated and living alone in Britain.

Judicial separations increased rapidly in the 1960s but as no figures are produced for unofficial separations, it is impossible to say whether this represented a real increase in total separations or not. Judicial separations are now uncommon because divorce is easier to obtain and both partners are more likely to accept divorce than in the past.

Empty-shell marriages

There are no reliable estimates of the number of empty-shell marriages. This is partly because it is very difficult to define empty-shell marriages and to operationalize any definition when conducting research.

However, impressionistic historical evidence does suggest that in the past people were more likely to accept an unsatisfactory marriage than today because divorce was almost impossible to obtain. For example, William Goode (1971) argues that empty-shell marriages were common in 19th-century America, when couples tended to stay together for the sake of their children and to preserve their social standing in the community.

Explanations for marital breakdown

According to Nicky Hart (1976), three types of factor can explain marital breakdown: value attached to marriage; degree of conflict between spouses; opportunities to escape from marriage.

The value of marriage

The functionalist Ronald Fletcher (1966) believed divorce has increased because people attach more value to marriage than in the past. If marriage is so important to individuals, they are more likely to seek divorce if their marriage is unsatisfactory. However, the British Social Attitudes Survey (2007) found that people do continue to value marriage but there is no evidence that the value attached has been increasing. Furthermore, cohabitation is increasingly accepted as an alternative to marriage.

Conflict between spouses

A number of possible reasons for increasing conflict between spouses:

- Functionalists such as Goode (1971) believe that conflict has increased because the nuclear family is becoming more isolated from other kin, placing an emotional burden on husbands and wives who have little support from other relatives.
- Dennis (1975) says that because the nuclear family specializes in fewer functions, husband–wife bonds are the main force holding the family together. If love goes, there is little to stop marital breakdown.
- Allan and Crowe (2001) believe marital breakdown has increased because the family is less likely to be an economic unit (for example running a family firm), making it easier for spouses to split up.

However, it shouldn't assume that conflict always leads to divorce. Economic strains after the 2008 financial crisis and recession did not lead to higher divorce perhaps because couples felt divorce would be too costly and destabilizing.

Essential notes

Operationalizing means the measurement of abstract concepts by defining them in research, for example by writing questionnaire questions. Divorce is easy to measure because it is defined legally, but separation and empty-shell marriages are harder to define and operationalize.

Examiners' notes

The problems of defining the different types of marital breakdown can be used to make the point that the validity of all of the statistics for measuring total marital breakdowns is open to question.

Examiners' notes

To get into the top mark band make some links between these points and functionalist theory in general.

Examiners' notes

You can develop Gibson's point further by linking it to the ideas of Beck and Giddens, whose theories suggest a similar relationship between modernity and changes in personal relationships (see p 21).

Modernity, freedom and choice

Colin Gibson (1994) links increased marital breakdown to modernity. He argues that individual competition and a free-market economy have placed increased emphasis on individualism. Individuals pursue personal satisfaction and are accustomed to the idea of consumer choice and fulfilment coming from such choice. Marriage is therefore treated like other consumer products and if it is not providing satisfaction it is more likely to be discarded.

The ease of divorce

Changing social attitudes have made it easier for people to contemplate divorce.

- Divorce has become more socially acceptable. The British and European Social Attitudes Survey (1998) found that 82% of people in Britain disagreed that married couples should stay together even if they didn't get along.
- Colin Gibson (1994) believes that secularization (the decline of religious belief) has loosened the rigid morality which in the past made divorce morally unacceptable to some people.
- Gibson also argues that society lacks shared values which may operate to stabilize marriage.

A wide range of laws have been introduced which make divorce both easier and cheaper to obtain. These laws have undoubtedly affected the divorce rate. For example, the Divorce Reform Act of 1971 removed the idea that one party had to be found guilty of some form of misbehaviour to allow divorce. This was followed by a large increase in divorce as more couples took advantage of the easier process of divorcing. Changing divorce laws are summarized in the table below.

Essential notes

It is important to learn some of the key dates and changes in legislation to give substance to longer answers on marital breakdown and the decline of the family. This will show that you understand that the changing rates of divorce might reflect changing laws as much as changing attitudes to marriage.

Legislation and date	Details of legislation	Consequences of legislation
Law before 1857	Divorce was only available through Acts of Parliament.	Divorce was too expensive for all but the most wealthy families so only a handful of divorces took place.
1857 Matrimonial Causes Act	The idea of matrimonial offence created, with adultery the main grounds for divorce.	Divorce became easier and cheaper to obtain but normally only if adultery could be established.
1950 Divorce Law	Grounds for divorce widened to include cruelty and desertion.	Divorce still based upon blaming one spouse for the breakdown of the marriage.

Divorce Reform Act 1971	Main grounds for divorce was now the 'irretrievable breakdown' of the marriage rather than actions of one spouse.	Made it much easier to obtain divorce without having to demonstrate that one partner had behaved badly.
Divorce Law 1984	Reduced the time before a divorce petition could take place from three years to one. Behaviour of partners to be taken into account in financial awards.	Made it quicker to get a divorce if the marriage was not successful.
Family Law Act 1996	It was no longer necessary to prove irretrievable breakdown, partners simply had to state that it had broken down. A period of reflection was introduced before divorce could be finalized, and greater use of mediation encouraged.	Aimed to increase the stability of marriage but made divorce easier in some ways.

Table 11
Changing divorce law

Divorce has become a more affordable proposition as a result of changes in laws which affect the cost of getting a divorce or provide support for those who have been divorced:

- In 1949 the Legal Aid and Advice Act provided for free advice for those who could not afford to pay a solicitor.
- The Child Support, Pensions and Social Security Act of 2000 laid down fixed contributions that absent parents had to pay for their children, making it easier for parents (usually the mother) to retain some economic security after divorce.

Conclusion

A rising divorce rate is just one of a range of social changes that seem to indicate a decline in the popularity of marriage. Others include a rising number of lone parents and single-person households, and an increase in cohabitation.

However, all these changes are open to interpretation, and Robert Chester (1985) says, 'on the evidence, most people will continue not only to spend most of their lives in a family environment, but also to place a high value on it'. Furthermore, high rates of remarriage after divorce suggest that it is particular marriages that many people are rejecting rather than the idea of marriage itself.

Jennifer Somerville (2000) points out that the vast majority of people in Britain still get married, most people live in a household headed by a married couple and extended kinship networks remain strong. She therefore concludes that rather than a simple decline in the institution of marriage, there has been a diversification of family forms and relationships.

Examiners' notes

Look out for 6-mark AS questions on reasons for increases in divorce and 10-mark questions at both AS and A level on factors shaping divorce rates.

Examiners' notes

You can use these contrasting views to add analysis and evaluation to 20-mark questions on these topics.

The life-cycle

The term **life-cycle** is often used to refer to the experiences of those passing through stages of life. The idea of the life-cycle is illustrated below.

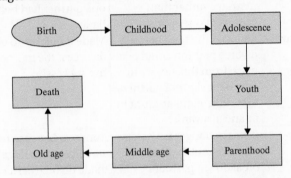

Fig 9
The life-cycle

The idea of the life-cycle implies there are set stages through which people pass.

An example of this approach to define an individual's progress is provided by the functionalist Talcott Parsons (1954). He saw people as passing through distinctive age groups with different social roles associated with each age group:

- Childhood, the period when **socialization** into society's culture takes place.
- Adolescence, when children begin to develop independence from their parents so that ultimately they can shift their allegiance from their parents to their marriage partner.
- Old age, which results in the loss of important social roles.

The life course

However, according to Jane Pilcher (1995), in reality there is no universal life-cycle because:

- Not everyone passes through every stage (for example, not everybody becomes a parent).
- Ageing is experienced differently within and between societies.

Pilcher therefore uses the term **life course** instead of life-cycle. She defines life course as 'a socially defined timetable of behaviours deemed appropriate for particular life stages within any one society'.

In different societies the life course will be seen differently; for example, in Western societies youthfulness may be valued more than in tribal societies. Even within a society it can be viewed differently; for example, women may value youthfulness more than men.

The life course is also affected by **life expectancy**. As life expectancy has increased in advanced Western societies, so perceptions of when middle age and old age start have changed.

Essential notes

The idea of the life course can be illustrated by using the material on childhood as a social construct, which is found on pp 54–55. As well as varying between societies, the nature of the life course changes over time as illustrated by changing conceptions of childhood.

Class, gender and the life course

Conflict perspectives such as Marxism and feminism emphasize inequality between different age groups, arguing that the life course is affected by wealth, income and access to resources. John Vincent (1995, 2006) believes that different classes and males and females experience ageing differently. For example, older women are more likely to experience life after retirement as a period of poverty and struggle because they generally have less entitlement to occupational pensions than men.

In general, Western capitalist societies attach more importance to age than other societies and being of working age has become increasingly important since this provides access to most people's main source of income – employment.

Age categories as a social construction

The idea of a fixed life-cycle is completely rejected by those who regard age categories as **socially constructed**. From this point of view, biological ageing has little or nothing to do with the expectations associated with different age groups. Society constructs these expectations and in doing so shapes what people believe to be normal behaviour.

Jenny Hockey and Allison James (1993) illustrate this approach in their research on old age. They believe old age is stereotyped in the media, and the elderly are treated as similar to children: old age is infantilized. For example, in old people's homes the elderly are allowed few choices so that they are marginalized, excluded and made dependent.

The postmodernists Featherstone and Hepworth (1991) believe that the life course has been **deconstructed** or has broken down. Clear-cut distinctions between age groups have become less and less important. **De-differentiation** has taken place where stages in the life-cycle have become less distinctive. They give the following examples:

- Children and adults have become less distinctive in the way they dress and in their leisure pursuits.
- Exposure to mass media means children are more aware of adult life.
- The middle class spend more on body maintenance to slow down ageing.
- Older people are more healthy and take more part in youthful lifestyles and leisure activities than in the past.

Featherstone and Hepworth conclude that **personal age** – how old people see themselves – is more important than **chronological age**, the number of years they have lived.

Examiners' notes

A useful tip for getting into the top mark band on many questions is to show you understand that there are differences in people's experiences based upon their class, gender, ethnicity and age. Mentioning this allows you to include extra evaluation if a perspective or theory emphasizes one of these differences more than others. (For example, feminists tend to emphasize gender to the exclusion of other social divisions.)

Examiners' notes

Featherstone and Hepworth can be included in any exam answers on postmodern theory, childhood or on questions about the changing relationships within the family.

Examiners' notes

The idea of families of choice can be linked to increasing family diversity.

Carol Smart: friends and family

Carol Smart (2007) believes that **personal life** is concerned with aspects of your life that involve choices that are made in the context of other people. With their emphasis on choice and personal meanings, Smart's ideas are partly based on those of the interactionist sociologist George Herbert Mead.

The focus on personal life stresses that people choose whom to associate with, so that friends can become more important than family members.

Smart emphasizes the idea of **families of choice** – that is, anybody can be seen as a member of your family, not just those who are related by blood or marriage.

Subjectivity and personal life

Unlike the relatively fixed view of families in traditional sociology of the family, personal life is likely to change constantly and is strongly linked to subjective areas of social life, including emotions, memories and feelings about bodies and sexuality.

It is also individual, based upon people's memories, their life history, the way their lives are embedded in the lives of others, how people relate to one another and how they use their imagination.

Key study

Carol Smart on the meaning of love

While some feminists feel love as a **patriarchal** concept that has no reality, Smart believes love can have a range of meanings depending upon the personal lives of different couples.

She conducted a study of 54 same-sex couples in a civil partnership and found that:

- 12 of the couples saw a civil partnership as *transforming the meaning of their love* and establishing it at a higher level, making it more real by pronouncing it in front of others and creating a more intense relationship.
- 37 of the couples saw the ceremony as the *culmination of their growing commitment* to one another. They emphasized their shared history and their survival through ups and downs. They related the ceremony more indirectly to love.
- 3 of the couples saw the ceremony as providing *external supports or props for their relationship*, helping to bond them together for the long term by committing to one another in the presence of other people.

All the couples saw it as important that friends and family knew about the ceremonies, showing that the emotions of personal life were bound up with relationships with others beyond their partner.

Essential notes

Smart's work is particularly useful for evaluating the theories of modernity put forward by Giddens (1992) and Back and Beck-Gernsheim (1995). Both claim that we live in a more individualized social world in which relationships are less important than they used to be.

Conclusion

Smart concludes that the study of personal life supports a 'connectedness thesis' showing how connections and relationships between people are crucial to understanding people's subjective lives and therefore their family and other personal relationships.

Jacqui Gabb: intimacy in families

Emotional life

Jacqui Gabb (2008) used qualitative methods to study the internal life of families, particularly the emotional life. She studied 24 participants from different types of family, including lone parent families, two-parent families, families from different class backgrounds and with different sexual orientations.

Gabb found that individuals could be attached to a wide range of people, including family and friends, and those who they lived with or who lived in other households.

She suggest that it is the 'quality of a relationship which is important not its functional purpose' and that these relationships are not necessarily limited to humans. Part of her study looked at pet–human relationships – pets can be just as important to personal life as relationships with other humans.

Physical touching was important in some intimate relationships (e.g. between mother and child), as well as between sexual partners and between humans and pets, but this can also cause anxiety in father–child relationships.

Intimate relationships involve strong emotional attachments at times, but they can also involve **power** differences, and there was considerable evidence in Gabb's study of intergenerational power struggle between parents and children.

Conclusion

The sociology of personal life suggests that sociological generalizations about changes in family life and relationships within families do not always do justice to the complex nature of those changes and relationships. Generally, the traditional sociology of the family neglects emotional aspects of personal lives and tends to underestimate the significance of friends and even pets in people's lives.

Examiners' notes

Gabb's study can be used to suggest limitations of traditional studies of conjugal roles and childhood in failing to take account of a full range of relationships (such as those with pets and friends) and in neglecting the role of emotions when measuring things like inequality and exploitation.

Types of conjugal role

Conjugal roles are the roles of husband and wife within marriage.

Two main types of conjugal role have been distinguished:

1. Segregated conjugal roles. The roles of husband and wife are very different. The husband is the main breadwinner and has little involvement with housework and childcare. Husbands tend to spend leisure time away from the family with male friends while women spend more time with female kin such as their mothers and sisters.

2. **Joint conjugal roles** involve men and women doing some paid work and also both spouses being involved with housework and childcare. Typically, with this type of conjugal role, men and women spend more time together and less time with their own groups of same sex friends.

These two types of conjugal role are extremes and often roles will be somewhere in between.

The symmetrical family

Young and Willmott (1973) claimed that joint conjugal roles were becoming more common in the symmetrical family. They found a move towards greater equality within marriage in that wives were now going out to work and husbands were providing more help with housework.

These views were heavily criticized by Ann Oakley (1974), who notes that in Young and Willmott's research a family was regarded as symmetrical if the husbands did any housework at least once a week. This hardly represented equality within a household. Her own research found that few men had high levels of participation in housework and childcare, with only 15% of men contributing significantly to the housework and 30% to the childcare.

Survey research on conjugal roles

Larger-scale research using survey methods provides more reliable data on the division of labour within the home. The British Social Attitudes Survey has collected data over a number of years and found some shift away from traditional roles in the 1980s and early 1990s. However, in more recent years there has been little change. In 1994 women always or usually did the laundry in 81% of households; by 2006 this had fallen just 4% to 77%.

Essential notes

Ann Oakley was a pioneering feminist sociologist who was the first to study housework systematically. She clearly showed the limitations of the work of Young and Willmott, who could be accused of putting forward malestream (mainstream, patriarchal) views. This research is dated now but more recent research provides some evidence that inequalities still exist.

Examiners' notes

Examiners will always be impressed with methodological evaluations of research. When using this or other survey research it is worthwhile mentioning that the reliability of the research is always questionable. For example, it has been demonstrated that men and women often given different answers when asked about who does household tasks, so it is difficult to know how reliable any set of figures is.

Individual reported as always/usually undertaking task	1994	2002	2006	2012
Does the laundry	%	%	%	%
Always/usually man	1	6	5	6
Both equally	18	15	17	20
Always/usually woman	79	78	74	70
Makes small repairs around the house	%	%	%	%
Always/usually man	75	71	73	75
Both equally	18	17	14	10
Always/usually woman	5	7	8	7

Cares for sick family members	%	%	%	%
Always/usually man	1	3	3	5
Both equally	45	36	44	38
Always/usually woman	48	48	43	36
Shops for groceries	%	%	%	%
Always/usually man	6	8	8	10
Both equally	52	45	47	43
Always/usually woman	41	45	41	44
Does the household cleaning	%	%	%	%
Always/usually man	n/a	5	6	8
Both equally	n/a	29	30	29
Always/usually woman	n/a	59	58	56

Table 12
Household tasks undertaken by men and women, 1994–2012

Childcare

Mary Boulton (1983) argues that who does which task does not adequately represent the burden of responsibility within households. She argues that even when men help more with childcare it is still mothers who take the main responsibility for their children and who have to prioritize their children above other aspects of their lives. The National Child Development Survey (1996) found it was still very unusual for fathers to take prime responsibility for childcare. A study of 70 families by Braun, Vincent and Ball (2011) found that in only three families were men mainly responsible for childcare.

Time

Another way to study gender roles is to examine time spent on different tasks. This gives an indication as to whether men or women spend more time on paid and unpaid work.

Gershuny (1999) examined data from 1974–1975 and 1997 to look at long-term trends. He found there had been a gradual shift towards men doing a higher proportion of housework, but in 1997 women continued to do more than 60% of the domestic work even when both partners were working.

The UK Time Use Survey (2005) found that women spent a total of 3 hours 32 minutes per day on housework and childcare whereas men spent on average 1 hour 56 minutes on these tasks. Men did however spend more time on paid employment. Nevertheless, on average, men had one hour 32 minutes per day more leisure time than women. The difference was less great for cohabiting men and women.

Table 13 below shows average minutes per person per day spent on various activities by sex.

2005	Male	Female
Cooking, washing up	27	54
Cleaning, tidying	13	47
Washing clothes	4	18

(continued)

Examiners' notes

Boulton's study can be used as an example of how the validity of research in this area can be questioned. Statistical data might not truly reflect the nature and extent of the burden of childcare for each parent.

Examiners' notes

Remember to point out some of the strengths of research as well as the weaknesses. Surveys such as this can be seen as relatively reliable because of their large sample size and the careful way in which samples are collected.

Table 13
Time spent on main activities with rates of participation by sex

2005	Male	Female
Repairs and gardening	23	11
Caring for own children	15	32
Paid work	211	132
Watching TV & Video	170	145

Essential notes

Conjugal roles will vary considerably between individual couples and social groups. For example, research generally shows that working-class marriages tend to be less equal than middle-class marriages and there will certainly be differences between ethnic groups in their conjugal roles.

Examiners' notes

In common with a number of other studies in this section you can gain extra marks by commenting on the unrepresentative nature of the sample. It is unlikely that dual-earner households in Nottingham will be entirely typical of the rest of the country.

Examiners' notes

Economic power is seen as particularly important both by Marxists and by Marxist-feminists. It is useful to make these theoretical links in answering questions on conjugal roles and also useful to use evidence such as this in answering theory questions on Marxism and feminism.

Conclusion

The evidence suggests there continue to be significant differences in the conjugal roles of husband and wife although the degree of inequality may be reducing over time. Men continue to do fewer household tasks, take less responsibility for childcare and have more leisure time than women. This could be caused by a combination of cultural factors (such as it being seen as 'unmanly' for men to do most of the housework) and economic factors (such as women having lower average pay than men).

Power and decision-making

The most common way to measure power in households is through an examination of decision-making.

A study by Hardill et al. (1997) examined power in dual-earner households in Nottingham using interviews. Households were classified into those where the husband's career took precedence in making major decisions, those where the wife's career took precedence, and those where neither career was deemed more important than the other. In 19 households the man's career came first, in five the woman's career came first and in six neither was prioritized. Thus men continued to be dominant in the majority of households.

Power and money

Power can also be measured in terms of control over money in the household. Jan Pahl (1989) studied 102 couples with children, and classified households into four types as shown in table 14.

Pahl found that wife-controlled pooling led to the most equal relationships but this pattern is most often found in low income households. Only just over a quarter of the couples had a system that was fairly equal, suggesting men continue to be dominant.

Research by Laurie and Gershuny (2000) using data from the British Household Panel Survey (1991 and 1995) showed movement away from the housekeeping allowance system which tends to make males dominant. Over the period the proportion saying that male and female partners had an equal say rose from 65% to 70%. Equality was more likely where women had high earnings, but overall men still have more economic power.

Pattern of management	Number of households	Type of decision-making	Degree of inequality
Husband-controlled pooling	39	Money was shared but the husband had the dominant role in choosing how it was spent	Gives men greater power
Wife-controlled pooling	27	Money was shared but the wife had the dominant role in choosing how it was spent	Gives women greater power

| Husband control | 22 | Husband usually had the only or main wage and gave his wife housekeeping money or allowance | Usually leads to male dominance |
| Wife control | 14 | Wife had overall control of the finances, perhaps giving her husband an allowance. Most typical in low income households which relied upon benefits | Appears to give women more power but in many cases they are struggling to pay the bills on low income making financial management a burden |

However, some sociologists such as Carol Smart (2007) argue that the meaning of money for individual couples is important and for some who controls the money is not a significant issue or an expression of power.

Table 14
Control over money in households – Jan Pahl

Conjugal roles and emotion work

Jean Duncombe and Dennis Marsden (1995) believe that any measurement of inequality within households must take account of **emotion work**. Emotion work involves thinking about the happiness and emotional well-being of others and acting in ways which will be of emotional benefit to others. It might include:

- complimenting other people
- smoothing over arguments
- buying presents and cards for birthdays
- smiling at a baby.

Duncombe and Marsden believe that women perform a **triple shift**, not only doing most of the housework and childcare, and doing their fair share of paid work, but also doing the vast majority of the emotion work. Their study involving interviews with 40 couples found that many women were dissatisfied with their partner's emotional input. Many believed that their emotion work helped to keep the family together.

Lesbian households

Gillian Dunne (1999) studied roles within lesbian households in many of which there was a dependent child. Unlike heterosexual households, responsibility for childcare was fairly equally shared rather than being largely the responsibility of one partner. Household tasks were also fairly equally shared in more than 80% of the cases studied.

Dunne concludes that masculine and feminine roles in society tend to lead to hierarchical relationships and male dominance. Without these gender roles greater equality is much easier to achieve.

Conjugal roles: conclusion

Most of the evidence suggests that women are still far from achieving equality within marriage in Britain today.

- They still do the majority of the housework.
- They still take the main responsibility for childcare.
- They still have less time for leisure than their male partners.

However, there is some evidence of change over time, and in terms of the total amount of hours per day spent on work of one kind or another differences between males and females are no longer that great.

Examiners' notes

This is a large-scale study so the data is quite reliable. It hints at the variety of relationships within households so remember to point out that there are a wide range of different arrangements affected by factors such as class and how much paid work each partner does.

Essential notes

This study and the concepts of the triple shift and emotion work have been widely quoted and it is important to learn them for the exam. The concept of emotion work adds an extra dimension to our understanding of family life although some people may feel that it is stretching the definition of work.

Types and definition

The main types of violence and abuse in families are:

- Violence and abuse perpetrated by one adult partner against another (usually called domestic violence).
- Violence and abuse perpetrated by adults against children (child abuse).

The Home Office (2000) defines domestic violence as 'any violence between current or former partners in an intimate relationship wherever and whenever it occurs. The violence may include physical, sexual, emotional, or financial abuse'.

This broad definition is generally given for domestic abuse. A narrower definition of domestic violence includes physical and sexual violence but not emotional or financial abuse.

The extent of domestic violence and abuse

The Crime Survey for England and Wales produces estimated figures on domestic violence and other forms of abuse. The 2014–15 survey found in the previous 12 months in England and Wales: there were an estimated 261,000 victims of domestic violence. Fig 10 shows that domestic violence rose considerably between 1981 and 1996, although it has declined in most years since then.

The 2009–10 Survey found that women were twice as likely as men to be victims of domestic violence (4% as opposed to 2%) and it also found that 7% of women aged 16 to 59 were victims of domestic abuse (physical, emotional, psychological or financial abuse) in the previous year compared with 4% of men.

Research by Nazroo (1999) suggests that domestic violence perpetrated by men against women tends to be more serious than that perpetrated by women on men, and women are likely to be much more fearful of the violence than men are.

Examiners' notes

You may be asked to define these terms for a 2-mark question.

Essential notes

The British Crime Survey is a government-funded self-report study in which people are asked if they have been the victims of crime.

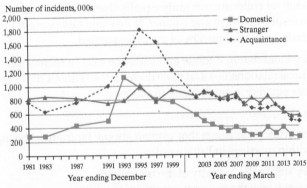

Fig 10
Trends in violent crime by type of perpetrator, 1981 to 2015 Crime Survey for England and Wales

This survey also found that 7% of women aged 16 to 59 were victims of domestic abuse (physical, emotional, psychological or financial abuse) in the previous year compared with 4% of men.

Research by Nazroo (1999) suggests that domestic violence perpetrated by men against women tends to be more serious than that perpetrated by women on men, and women are likely to be much more fearful of the violence than men are.

The British Crime Survey is based on a large sample of over 40,000 so it is quite reliable, but it only covers England and Wales and people aged 16 or over so the scope of the statistics is somewhat limited. The validity of the data may be open to question since it can be a matter of interpretation whether abuse has taken place.

Explanations of domestic violence and abuse

Feminism

Radical feminists, such as Erin Pizzey (1974), see domestic violence as resulting from patriarchy. In a male-dominated or patriarchal society, men use violence or the threat of violence in order to control women. Pizzey also argues that domestic violence is widely tolerated and often not seen as a serious crime. Patriarchal values lead to female partners being seen as essentially the property of their male partners, and therefore using violence to control them is seen as partially acceptable.

Fiona Brookman (2008) believes that the nature of **masculinity** is partly to blame. In our culture masculinity values control over others, so men can resort to violence if they feel they are losing control over their female partner. Her research was based on in-depth interviewing with violent men.

A problem with this approach is that it does not explain the existence of domestic violence perpetrated by women against men. Social attitudes may also have changed since Pizzey was writing, with domestic violence now seen as less socially acceptable by the public, and more likely to result in prosecution by the police.

Dysfunctional families

Some conservative commentators associated with the views of the New Right/neoliberals believe that domestic violence takes place in **dysfunctional families**, that is, families which do not function well. Their view is that violence results from the instability of families caused by factors such as increasing cohabitation and divorce, and the decline in moral standards in some families, particularly those from lower social classes. This view suggests that feminists exaggerate male violence and underestimate female violence.

This approach is criticized by feminists who believe that male violence against women is both much more serious and much more common than female violence against men.

Emotional intensity and family life

Anthony Giddens (2006) argues that it is the nature of family life that makes domestic violence quite common. Family life is characterized by 'emotional intensity and personal intimacy', meaning that it is normally charged with strong emotions, often 'mixing love and hate'. In these circumstances, even minor arguments can escalate into acts of violence. The increasing isolation of the nuclear family from extended kinship networks may be increasing this intensity.

A problem with this approach is that it does not explain why violence is common in some families but not others.

Essential notes

It is useful to comment that these figures may underestimate the true extent of domestic violence and abuse, since many victims may be unwilling to admit that it has taken place.

Examiners' notes

It is useful to comment here that liberal feminists recognize that there may have been some improvements in the treatment of victims of domestic abuse and violence. Referring to different feminist perspectives can help to get you in the top mark band.

Examiners' notes

To critique this view you can suggest that there is little evidence to support it and it may be based largely on the political views of the writers.

Examiners' notes

You can gain extra credit by making reference to specific research on changes in extended family networks, either to support or criticize this view (see pp 16–17).

The dominant framework

Michael Wyness (2006) says that commonsense thinking sees childhood as 'a natural and inevitable phase of life that we all go through'. It is seen as a biological state due to the physical and mental immaturity of children. Therefore, childhood should be the same across different cultures and over time.

Prout and James (1997) see this view as the dominant framework.

Child	Adult
Nature	Culture
Simple	Complex
Amoral	Moral
Asocial	Social
Person-in-waiting	Personhood
Becoming	Being

Table 15
The dominant framework

The key features of this framework for Wyness are:

1. Childhood and adulthood are seen as opposites, and childhood is seen as lacking the key attributes of being a person which are attained in adulthood.
2. Children are not seen in their own rights but in terms of what they will become later, that is, they are seen as future adults.
3. Children are regarded as at the earliest or most primitive stage of individuality.

Prout sees this view of children as the product of modernity. In modernity adults are associated with rationality and children are associated with a lack of rationality.

The dominant framework is backed up by **developmentalism** in which childhood is seen as a series of stages through which children develop as they get closer to adulthood.

Childhood as a social construction

Many sociologists challenge the dominant framework by claiming that childhood is a social construction. From this viewpoint it is not a natural, biological stage in development but a social role which is learnt through **socialization** and which varies from society to society and over time. For example:

- In some societies children do a considerable amount of paid work.
- Amnesty International (2007) estimates there are 300,000 child soldiers in the world.
- Pilcher (1995) identifies wide cultural variations in the role of children. Samoan children are expected to take part in physical and dangerous work, and in Tikopia in the Pacific children are not expected to obey adults.

Essential notes

Useful links can be made here with the theories of modernity and changes in relationship put forward by Beck and Giddens (see p 21).

Essential notes

The idea of a social construction is a crucial one and may need defining in the exam. When sociologists say something is a social construction they mean that it is shaped by a society's culture even when people might believe that it is natural and is not influenced by social factors.

Key study

Philippe Ariès – centuries of childhood

Ariès (1973) pioneered the idea of childhood as a social construction. According to his research, in mediaeval times (roughly the 12th to 16th centuries) modern conceptions of childhood did not exist. For example:

- Chronological age (the number of years since you were born) was not considered significant.
- Children often died before reaching adulthood and so were regarded as being less important than they are today.
- Parents kept the mourning for children who died to a minimum.
- Children were expected to work as soon as they were physically capable of doing so.
- Both adults and children spent time on play and often played the same games.
- There were few specialist clothes for children so they dressed like little adults.
- Children were not regarded as being especially innocent, nor protected from exposure to sexuality.

Examiners' notes

This is the most important study that needs to be quoted if you are asked questions about the nature of childhood or changes in childhood over long periods of time. Some sociologists don't agree with Ariès about the exact reasons for changes in childhood or the timing of the changes (see the evaluation below) but it's widely accepted that his general view is broadly correct.

Evaluation

Ariès has been criticized for claiming that there was no concept of childhood in mediaeval times; others believe the conception of childhood was simply different. He has also been criticized for basing his research on a small sample of untypical French aristocratic families.

The emergence of childhood

Ariès believes that towards the end of the mediaeval period modern conceptions of childhood began to appear as church leaders began to see children as 'fragile creatures who needed to be safeguarded and reformed'. The introduction of schools, in which separate age groups were taught and children were segregated from the adult world, helped introduce the idea of childhood as a distinct phase of life in which children had to be kept innocent and protected from the adult world.

Compared with medieval times, society became more **child-centred** with the well-being and development of children seen as very important. In the 20th century, sciences such as psychology, psychoanalysis and paediatrics were developed, and these created specialists who emphasized the needs of children.

Examiners' notes

The idea of child-centredness is an important one for questions about changing roles within the family because it implies changes in the roles of parents and children.

As modern attitudes to childhood developed, children were:

- treated differently according to their chronological age
- seen as important and in need of protection
- strongly mourned if they died
- not required to work
- given specialist games and toys which adults did not take part in
- given distinctive clothes
- seen as asexual and kept away from exposure to sexuality.

Edward Shorter – childhood and the modern family

Edward Shorter (1976) uses a wider range of evidence than Ariès, and from a greater variety of countries, to describe and explain the development of childhood.

Shorter links the development of childhood to motherhood. According to his research, in the 17th and early 18th centuries mothers showed little interest in bonding with their children and could handle children quite roughly. Children were usually left to cry rather than picked up and comforted.

Attitudes started changing in the 18th century because:

1. The idea of romantic love began to develop and children were seen as the products of a special relationship.
2. Philosophers such as Jean Jacques Rousseau popularized the idea that children were born good and could become reasoning adults if successfully socialized.
3. New ideas began to circulate on the best ways to raise children.

By the 20th century, being a 'good' mother was considered very important and the harshness of early centuries was replaced with a desire to nurture children. Mothers developed a sacrificial role in which their children's lives were more important than their own.

Evaluation

Shorter assumes that changing ideas were largely responsible for changes in childhood. However some sociologists believe that other factors were more important.

Other explanations of the development of childhood

- Neil Postman (1982) sees the explanation for changes in childhood as lying in technological change. The printing press developed in the late 15th century and as a result learning to read became increasingly important in society. Learning to read was a gradual process and required extended schooling of children. This led to the separation of adults and children and the idea that children had to pass through age-related stages as they progressed towards adulthood.
- Other sociologists believe that Postman attaches too much importance to a single cause of the changes. Jane Pilcher (1995) also sees employment legislation as important. In the 19th century, Factory Acts banned children from an increasing number of workplaces, and this laid the foundation for the separation of adults and children in schools. Pilcher believes that the development of childhood varied for different groups, such as different social classes and boys and girls, but eventually the modern idea of childhood developed for all children.

Examiners' notes

You can use Shorter to contrast with Ariès (see p 55) in answering questions on the social construction of childhood or changes in childhood. Shorter provides a more developed explanation than Ariès and uses a greater variety of evidence, but Shorter himself has been criticized (see below).

Examiners' notes

Evaluation of these theories is really important to get into the higher mark bands on essay questions. Contrasting the competing viewpoints is an effective way to evaluate.

Childhood and modernity

Christopher Jenks (2005) believes that the development of modern childhood involves a shift from the **Dionysian image of the child** to the **Apollonian image**.

- The Dionysian image assumes that children naturally pursue their own pleasure, which can lead to their acting in evil ways. They therefore require close control and strict moral guidance to grow up to be moral adults. From this viewpoint there was little sentimentality about children so that having young children working in mines and factories and as chimney sweeps was quite acceptable.
- The Apollonian image developed from the middle of the 18th century, based on the ideas of Rousseau. It believed that children are born good but this good side must be coaxed out of them sympathetically. This thinking resulted in the idea of child-centred education and the banning of paid work for young children. Harsh physical punishment was replaced by monitoring and careful control of where children were allowed to go and what they were allowed to do. For example, much of children's time was spent in school behind school desks.

Examiners' notes

These concepts might seem rather obscure and remote from social life, but they do underpin attitudes to children and you can certainly get credit for using concepts such as these.

Childhood and postmodernity

Jenks believes that postmodern childhood has developed. In postmodern societies identities have been destabilized so that people no longer have a secure, grounded sense of who they are. Class solidarity has broken down and family life is insecure with frequent divorce. In these circumstances children have become the final source of **primary relationships** – the most fulfilling and unconditional relationships. Wives and husbands and partners have become disposable, but children are not and the parent–child bond is therefore the most important in society. This intensifies the sense that children need to be protected, and helps to explain the growing anxiety about child abuse. Children become subject to increased surveillance because parents are more fearful for their children and determined to protect them.

Evaluation

Jenks has been criticized for ignoring evidence that mothers place increasing emphasis on careers rather than children, but research by Gatrell (2005) found than many parents do see relationships with children as more important than their relationship with their partner.

Essential notes

Jenks' views are very similar to those of Anthony Giddens (see p 21) and it is worth mentioning this. Both Jenks and Giddens offer rather generalized views without much research to back them up. Both of them neglect the variations in relationships within families, for example between different ethnic groups.

Neil Postman: the disappearance of childhood

Postman (1994) claims that the distinction between childhood and adulthood has been eroded in recent years so that childhood no longer exists as a distinct stage in the life course.

He explains the disappearance in the following ways:

1. The growth of the mass media has exposed children to the adult world. It is easy for them to access images of sex and they can view suffering and death on television news programmes. More recently, the internet provides children with access to images and information from which they were previously sheltered.
2. The difference between adulthood and childhood is increasingly blurred. Examples of this include:
   - children dressing in more adult and sometimes more sexualized ways
   - adults trying to dress and act in more youthful ways
   - the lack of a clear-cut transition to adulthood as adolescence is extended and young people often delay getting a job, setting up their own home, getting married and having children.

Children as consumers

Another way in which the distinctiveness of childhood may be disappearing is in the increasing participation of children in consumption. Research by Evans and Chandler (2006) found there was strong peer pressure amongst children to persuade their parents to buy them the latest designer goods. Marketing and adverts are often aimed at children and encourage participation in consumer society.

Jenks – the continuing distinctiveness of childhood

Jenks (2005) accepts that there is increasing confusion over the nature of childhood but he does not believe that it is disappearing as a distinct stage in the life course. He does, though, agree that there has been increased concern about the loss of innocence amongst children since the 1993 murder of the toddler James Bulger by two older children in Liverpool.

Nevertheless, Jenks points out that children continue to be highly regulated and restricted by laws which control behaviour in public spaces, the consumption of alcohol and cigarettes, education, sexuality, political rights and so on. Table 16 below shows the ages at which various activities are legal in the UK.

Table 16
Legal ages in the UK

At any age you can:	At 5 you can:	At 10 you are:	At 12 you can:	At 13 you can:
Agree to or refuse medical treatment. Open a bank account. Ask to see school records. Have confidential contraceptive treatment.	See a U or PG film by yourself.	Legally responsible for any crimes.	Buy a pet. See a 12-rated film by yourself.	Work part time.

At 14 you can:	At 16 you can:	At 17 you can:	At 18 you can:	At 21 you can:
Go into a pub alone for soft drinks with the landlord's consent. Work in a market.	Have a beer with a meal in a restaurant. Buy lottery tickets. Marry or join the armed forces with parental agreement. Have sex. Ride a moped.	Give blood. Drive a motorcycle, car or van. Apply for a helicopter pilot's licence.	Buy alcohol. Buy cigarettes. Serve on a jury. Leave home, join the armed forces or marry without parental permission. Buy fireworks. Place bets. Own land. Vote.	Become a local councillor or MP. Drive larger lorries.

Theoretical approaches to childhood: the conventional approach

The conventional theoretical approach to children and childhood reflects the views of functionalists and the New Right/neoliberals. This sees children as a vulnerable group in need of protection from exposure to adult life. It views children as growing up too quickly and therefore being likely to engage in inappropriate behaviour.

An example of this approach is provided by Melanie Phillips (1997), a right-wing commentator who believes that parenting culture in Britain is failing children. She claims that:

1. Liberal ideas of parenting have given children too many rights and powers and have prevented parents from disciplining their children (e.g. through smacking) to ensure that they show respect for parents and others in authority.
2. **Peer groups** and the mass media have come to have more influence on children than parents and teachers, leading to children losing their innocence and becoming sexualized at a younger age (e.g. the increase in pregnancies under 16).

Berry Mayall – the new sociology of children

Berry Mayall (2004) has a very different view to Phillips, arguing that most ideas on childhood and children are **adultist** – they see children from an adult point of view and are biased in favour of adults at the expense of children. According to Mayall this ignores the rights of children and underestimates the ability of children to think and act for themselves.

Now that women have achieved greater rights, children are the final group who are denied rights to make their own decisions. Children have no right to shape their own schooling and have little influence on policies which affect them. This exposes children to danger, for example making it easy for adults to abuse them.

By giving children more of a voice in policies which affect them they will be better served by social policies and less vulnerable to abuse. Given that widespread physical and sexual abuse of children has been uncovered in recent years, Mayall's approach seems particularly valuable.

Essential notes

As noted earlier, these sort of New Right/neoliberal views tie in with some of Postman's ideas.

Examiners' notes

Mayall is useful for adding a critical view which can be contrasted with all the other approaches to childhood and children. You could even suggest that her pioneering perspective will gain increasing acceptance in sociology, rather like the way in which feminism has gained acceptance for female viewpoints. Therefore, try to use this material in answering questions about the changing roles of children.

Demography

The study of demography examines factors affecting the total size of the population in a country. Total population size is shaped by the following factors:

1. The birth rate – the number of live births per thousand of the population per year.
2. The fertility rate – the number of live births per thousand women aged 15 to 44 per year.
3. The **death rate** – the number of deaths per thousand of the population per year.
4. Migration – the number of people entering a country (immigration) and the number of people leaving the country (emigration). Net migration refers to the difference between the numbers entering and leaving the country.

The population of the UK

In 1801 the UK had a population of 10.5 million. By 1901 it had risen to 37 million, by 1971 to just under 56 million, and it was estimated at 65 million in 2015.

Fig 11 shows the total number of births and deaths in the UK since 1901. There have been fewer deaths than births in the UK in every year since 1901, with the exception of 1976. This has meant that the population has risen largely as a result of natural increase for most of the 20th century, although migration has also played a part, especially in more recent years (see pp 66–67). Natural increase occurs when the number of births exceeds the number of deaths. In the 1950s, for example, natural change accounted for 98% of population growth; however, in 2015 net migration explained approximately two-thirds of the increasing UK population.

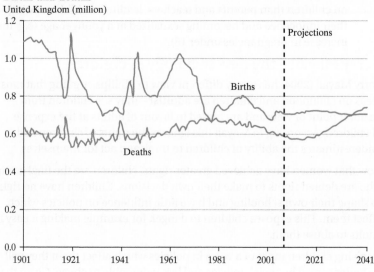

Births and deaths
United Kingdom (million)

Fig 11
UK births and deaths from 1901

The birth rate

There has been a long-term decline in the number of births in the UK and also in the birth rate.

In 2008 there were 790 000 live births in the UK compared with 1 093 000 in 1901 when the population was significantly lower. Although there have been fluctuations in the birth rate, which increased with a 'baby boom' after both the First and Second World Wars (partly because some people had delayed starting families until after the ending of the wars), over the long term the birth rate has been declining.

The fertility rate

Much of the decline in the birth rate has been the result of a declining fertility rate – women are choosing to have fewer children. The total fertility rate (the number of children each woman has) declined from 3.5 in 1900 to 1.7 in 1997. It rose slightly to 1.82 in 2014.

This recent rise in fertility is partly due to patterns of migration with immigrants to the UK tending to have slightly larger families than non-immigrants. The recent rise has also been explained in terms of rising fertility rates in older women, some of which may be due to improvements in fertility treatments such as IVF.

Reasons for the long-term decline in birth and fertility rates

Examiners' notes

If you are asked for a long answer about reasons for changes in population size, you will need to discuss births, deaths and migration to give an overall picture. You can also discuss sociological theory on why demographic changes may have occurred, to help you develop the answer.

Total Fertility Rate

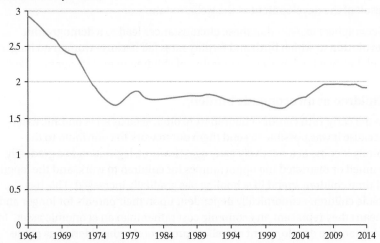

Fig 12
Falling fertility rates from 1964 to 2014 in the UK

Changes in gender roles

A major part of the decline can be explained in terms of women choosing to have fewer children. As their role in society has changed, many women are choosing to delay childbearing and to limit the number of children they have. Factors include:

- Improved contraception from the 1960s, which gave women more control over their own fertility.

- Easier access to abortion.
- Women are less likely to get married than in the past and cohabiting women are less likely to have children than married women.
- An increase in the number of women in paid employment, particularly after marriage, so that more women delay or limit childbearing to fit in with careers.
- In dual-earner families it is more difficult to combine work with care of a large number of children.
- More opportunities for women in employment because of the growth of the service sector.
- Greater legal equality for women, such as the Equal Pay Act (1970) which has made working more worthwhile.
- Improved female performance in education and increasing educational opportunities.

A decline in the birth and fertility rates may be largely a matter of choice, particularly the choice of women. Also, women who delay the birth of their first child until they are relatively old may not remain fertile long enough to have large numbers of children. However, fertility rates amongst older age groups have been rising.

Falling infant mortality

The **infant mortality rate** (the number of children dying before their first birthday per thousand live births) has fallen dramatically as a result of factors such as rising living standards, improved hygiene and sanitation, improvements in healthcare, and improved monitoring of child welfare as a result of the development of the welfare state.

Geographers explain that these circumstances lead to a **demographic revolution** in which birth and fertility rates fall because women no longer feel they need to have a large number of children to protect against the risk of infant mortality.

Children as an economic burden

In the early 19th century children were often seen as an economic asset because it was possible to send them out to work to contribute to the family income at a relatively early age. However, legislation has gradually banned or restricted the opportunities for children to work, and the length of time children spend in schooling has gradually increased. This has made children economically dependent upon their parents for longer and means they represent an economic cost rather than an economic asset. In addition, the development of welfare provision for the elderly has made parents less dependent upon children for care and support in old age. As people expect and desire rising living standards, then there is a greater disincentive to have large numbers of children.

Changing attitudes

As pages 54–73 show, attitudes towards children and childhood have changed. Families and society in general have become more child-centred, more concerned with the well-being of children, than they were in the past. As social norms about what constitutes adequate childcare have changed, the time and costs involved in raising children have increased. This has further reduced the economic attractiveness of having large numbers of children. Instead, parents are more likely to concentrate their efforts on raising a small number of children as well as they can.

Beck and Beck-Gernsheim (1995) believe that these changes are linked to a process of individualization. People no longer have to follow traditional norms and values and instead make their own decisions. These decisions include: whether or not to get married, whether to stay married and whether to have children. Uncertainty and the risk of relationship breakdown make people wary of having too many children. Ironically, however, the children that people do have become increasingly important to them since parent–child relationships are permanent while marriages may be temporary.

The effects of changes in fertility

Changes in fertility can have a number of consequences for society. These include.

- Changes in the **dependency ratio**. The dependency ratio is the ratio between the economically productive part of the population and non-workers, or dependents, such as children and the elderly. Falling fertility rates reduce the number of dependent children in the short term but in the long term lead to fewer adults of working age, which can increase the proportion of the population who are dependent.
- Effects on public services such as education. Falling numbers of births can lead to the closure of maternity units and schools, which can create problems if the birth rate increases later.
- Falling fertility can contribute further to changes in gender roles, giving women more time to devote to their careers and therefore contributing to greater equality in conjugal relationships.

Essential notes

This material on variations in the death rate can be used to make the important point that social factors play a crucial role in life expectancy and death rates.

Changes in the death rate and life expectancy

- Since 1901 the total number of deaths in the UK has remained relatively stable at around the 600,000 mark. In 1901 there were 632,000 deaths and 574,700 in 2007. The peak year for deaths since 1901 was in 1918 when approximately 690,000 people died, with an influenza outbreak and the First World War claiming many of those lives.
- Since 1901, however, the UK population has increased, therefore the death rate has fallen, although there was a rise between 2014 and 2015 suggesting that the fall in the death rate might not be sustained in the long term.
- In 1900–1902 death rates stood at 18.4 per thousand per year, by 1976 this was 12.1. Between 1976 and 2007 death rates fell by more than 22% to 9.4 per thousand per year, and it was 8.9 in 2012.
- **Infant mortality rates** (number of babies dying before the age of one per thousand babies born alive per year) have declined even quicker than overall death rates, falling by two thirds from 14.5 in 1976 to 3.8 in 2013 – the lowest ever recorded.
- Falling death rates are reflected in rising life expectancy. In 1901 life expectancy at birth was 45 for boys and 49 for girls; by 2014 this had reached 81.4 years, 83.2 years for girls and 79.5 years for boys.
- Death rates and life expectancy vary between social groups and places. For example, government statistics showed that in 2013 infant mortality was more than twice as high in children of married couples from the lowest class (routine occupations), at 5.4%, than it was for children from the highest class (higher managerial and large employers), at 2.2%.

Reasons for the declining death rate and rising life expectancy

Developments in medicine

A variety of researchers have found that well over half of the decline in the death rate since the 19th century has been due to a decrease in infectious diseases such as tuberculosis, measles, whooping cough and diphtheria. The most obvious reason for this decline is medical advances. From the 1920s vaccines were introduced to combat many of these diseases, and antibiotics were introduced from the 1930s. However, Thomas McKeown (1979) argues that most of the fall in deaths from infectious diseases took place before the discovery of vaccinations and antibiotics. He believes that improved nutrition was the most important factor in reducing death rates from such diseases, with improvements in hygiene accounting for about 20% of the decline.

More recently, death rates from the so-called 'diseases of affluence' such as cancer and heart disease have increased. For these diseases medical knowledge and improved medical services have made a difference. For example, deaths from heart disease have decreased partly as a result of the availability of better drugs and operations such as heart bypass.

Improvements in maternity care since the establishment of the NHS in 1949 have probably made a significant difference to infant mortality rates.

Examiners' notes

This is very important and useful research because it successfully challenges common sense assumptions about the reasons for the falling death rate, so make sure you have learned the details for use in the exam.

Nutrition and living standards

Studies by Rowntree and others (1899, 1950) demonstrated a rapid decline in **absolute poverty** (absolute poverty involves a lack of the basic necessities of life such as food and shelter). Increases in living standards have allowed significant improvements in diet throughout the population. Better nutrition helps to increase to infectious diseases.

Welfare, health and environment

At the same time as individual living standards have risen, government provision of welfare and health has improved.

- In the late 19th and early 20th centuries significant improvements were made in the water supply and sewage disposal.
- In 1914 free school meals were introduced for those who could not afford them.
- Sickness benefit was introduced in 1911.
- After the Beveridge Report of 1944, the range of welfare provision expanded and became more universally available. It provided protection against risk factors such as old age through pensions, and low income through housing benefits, unemployment benefit and the benefit now called Income Support.

Lifestyle changes

There have been substantial reductions in smoking which will gradually feed through to a lowering death rate. There has also been growing awareness of the benefits of healthy eating, regular exercise and limiting alcohol intake.

However, this might have been counteracted by increasing levels of obesity and social factors (such as changes in work and growing car ownership) which have led to less active lifestyles than in the past.

A reversal of the trend?

In 2015 the number of deaths rose 5.4% in England compared with the previous year, following on from smaller rises between 2010 and 2014.

Danny Dorling (2016) suggested that the rise might be due to:

- cuts in the provision of healthcare to the elderly in the NHS, particularly during winter
- Severe cuts in social services leading to less provision of services such as meals on wheels.

Others attributed the rise partly to increased mortality from flu, but the trend does suggest that further declines in the death rate cannot be guaranteed without better funding of the welfare state.

Conclusion

Most of the reduction in the death rate is due to improvements in living standards and the expansion of welfare although medical advances have come to play a greater role in recent years as the significance of infectious diseases has declined. The continued inequalities in death rates between social classes show that economic and social factors continue to be important and suggest that growing inequality and cuts to the welfare state could lead to sustained increases in the number of deaths and the death rate.

Essential notes

This doesn't mean that there is no longer any poverty. **Relative poverty** (that is, being poor relative to other people in a society) remains a major problem and research shows that it lowers life expectancy. Absolute poverty lowers it even more, and is still experienced by a few: for example, some of the homeless.

Examiners' notes

Don't forget to learn some of these details, but be careful not to use older examples if the question specifies a shorter timeframe (for example, the last 30 years).

Introduction

Net migration is the difference between the number of long-term immigrants entering and the number of long-term migrants leaving a country.

Migration has become a highly political issue in recent years in the UK with the numbers of immigrants from EU countries being a significant issue in the 2016 referendum on whether the UK should leave the EU (Brexit).

Patterns of migration

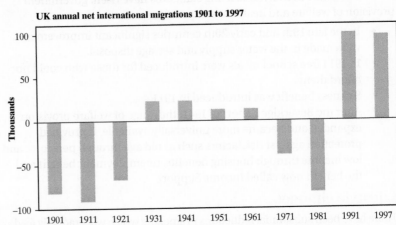

UK annual net international migrations 1901 to 1997

Fig 13
Patterns of net international migration to and from the UK each decade from 1901 to 1997

Essential notes

It is important to emphasize that there have been long periods when there were more emigrants from Britain than immigrants to Britain, but recently the reverse has been true.

Fig 13 shows that:

- In the early decades of the 20th century the UK was a net exporter of people. The majority of those leaving went to the USA, Australia, New Zealand and other colonies. Most immigrants were from Ireland. After the end of the First World War the trend reversed with many migrants returning to Britain and the immigration of Eastern European Jews fleeing persecution.
- From the late 1950s immigration from the Caribbean and the Asian subcontinent increased, although in the 1970s and 1980s Britain was a net exporter of people as UK citizens left to start new lives in Australia, New Zealand and South Africa.
- In recent decades immigration has exceeded emigration despite a variety of Acts restricting the rights of Commonwealth citizens to settle in Britain. Some immigrants are asylum seekers fleeing persecution, and most recently many are from European Union countries, particularly in Eastern Europe. Some British people have emigrated to live in other European countries, often for retirement purposes. The European Union allows free movement of people within its boundaries. In 2004, the European Union was expanded to include 10 new member states including Poland. There have also been some illegal immigrants.

- In 2010 David Cameron, then Conservative Prime Minister, said he would like to reduce net immigration to the 'tens of thousands' but by the year to July 2016 it stood at 336,000. This was widely seen as an important factor in the referendum decision for Britain to leave the EU in June 2016. Membership of the EU involves the acceptance of the free movement of workers between member countries.

It remains to be seen what rules will be introduced on migration after The Brexit vote, but patterns of migration are always changing and the vote itself might make emigration to the UK a less attractive proposition and emigration from the UK to EU countries more difficult. These factors will affect future population changes.

Usually migrants tend to be relatively young and they are more likely to be male than female. However, older people may also emigrate, for example British people seeking to retire in warmer countries such as France and Spain.

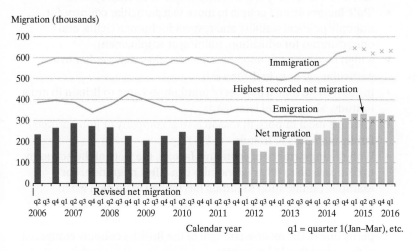

Fig 14
UK migration 2006–2016

Factors affecting migration

Legislation and border control

Legal migration is affected by laws governing the right of people to move to other countries, while illegal migration is affected by the attempts of states to control access to their territory. For example, the UK has limited immigration from the Caribbean and Asian subcontinent due to Acts such as the 1962 and 1968 Commonwealth Immigration Acts. The 1999 Immigration and Asylum Act tightened up regulations allowing asylum seekers to settle in Britain. However, the expansion of the European Union gave more people the right to come to Britain.

At the time of writing, it was unclear how regulation would change as the Conservative government under Theresa May sought to reduce net immigration to under 100,000.

Globalization

Globalization involves a process in which national boundaries become less important and interconnections between different parts of the globe become more important. With the development of mass communications, awareness and understanding of other countries and cultures has increased. With rapid, cheap and safe transport systems such as jet air travel, movement around the globe has become more affordable and easier. These factors have increased the total amount of migration in the world and make it difficult to control migration entirely. For example, refugees from war zones such as Syria are more like to travel some distance to claim asylum.

'Push' and 'pull' factors

Other factors which affect migration can be seen as 'push' and 'pull' factors.

- **'Push' factors** give people a reason to emigrate. For example, they may be fleeing war persecution, poverty or unemployment.
- **'Pull' factors** attract people to move to a particular country, for example political stability and respect for human rights, and opportunities for education, training or employment.
- A high proportion of migrants state that they move either to a particular job or to look for work.
- In 2007, more than a quarter of immigrants came to Britain in order to study. Many would later leave.
- The next most important reason is to accompany or join partners, family members or friends.
- With the importance of economic factors, the state of the economy in comparison to other economies can affect migration. For example, immigration to Britain has tended to be high when employment opportunities are greater than in other countries. For example, net migration to Britain before the Brexit vote was high partly due to the relative strength of the British economy compared with many other EU countries.

Examiners' notes

You must discuss both these types of factor in longer answers but it isn't really possible to say which is more important because this varies with individual circumstances.

Essential notes

Economic factors can act as both a push and a pull for migrants; for example, if there are few jobs in their country of origin but more jobs available in the country they are emigrating to.

Social networks

Raghuram and Erel (2014) argue that thinking in terms of push–pull factors neglects the role of social networks in patterns of migration. Much migration takes places in groups (whether family groups of groups of friends) and/or to move to a place where friends or family are already living. This approach takes more account of the emotional costs and benefits of migration – costs and benefits which are difficult to quantify. It also helps to explain why migrants may come in clusters in terms of places of origin and in some cases where they migrate to.

Historical and structural factors

Raghuram and Erel (2014) also argue that analysis in terms of what they call historical-structural factors. Globalization is one general factor of this type, but more specific issues of economic and political power are also important. States might encourage or restrict migration in order to further the power of the state, and governments might follow particular migration policies to increase their own popularity. In the UK, for example, migration rules take account of income and wealth in determining who can live in the UK, and the EU has a fundamental rule requiring free movement that is linked to a political desire for greater European integration. Rich and powerful countries and their citizens tend to be subject to more liberal migration rules from other countries than poorer countries and their citizens are.

Conclusion

Future patterns of migration to and from the UK are very unpredictable given the uncertainty over the economic, political and social consequences of the Brexit vote, but as a result of globalization (see below) it seems likely that migration will remain at high levels in the world as a whole.

The definition and extent of globalization

Globalization involves a process in which national boundaries become less important and interconnections between different parts of the globe become increasingly so. With the development of mass communications, awareness and understanding of other countries and cultures has increased. With rapid, cheap and safe transport systems such as jet air travel, movement around the globe has become easier and more affordable. This has facilitated an increase in the total amount of migration in the world and changes in the nature of migration.

In 2015 the UN estimated there were 244 million international migrants in 2015, which is a rise of 71 million since the year 2000.

An 'Age of Migration'

The extent of migration has become so great that Castles and Miller (2009) argue that we have entered an 'Age of Migration' in which global migration is taking on some new characteristics. These involve:

- A genuine globalization of migration, so that more countries have significant numbers of emigrants and immigrants, and in each country immigrants are likely to come from an increasingly wide range of countries.
- Increasing differentiation of migrants, with many different types of migrants arriving in most countries. In the UK this includes permanent migrants, temporary workers and refugees.
- A feminization of migration, so that most migrants are no longer male and there is more balance between the sexes. For example, there are now more female workers becoming migrant, e.g. Filipinos going to the Middle East and Thais to Japan.
- An acceleration of migration, with the amount of migration continually increasing.
- A politicization of migration, with the issue becoming increasingly contested, controversial and subject to political debate (e.g. the Brexit vote in the UK and the issue of refugees in Eastern and southern Europe). There are political controversies between those who believe that high levels of immigration can undermine the cultural identity of the nation and those who welcome a growing cosmopolitanism (the coexistence of ethnic, religious and national identity within the population).

Super-diversity

Steve Vertovec (2007) goes further, arguing that a '**super-diversity**' of migration has developed. This involves the rapid growth of migration of different ethnic groups and nationalities, and within those groups migrants with different legal statuses (e.g. migrants married to citizens of a country, migrants who are refugees, and asylum seekers who are permanent or temporary migrants).

Examiners' notes

You can evaluate the idea of the 'Age of Migration' by pointing out that mass migration is not new, but that perhaps it occurs in more parts of the world than it did in the past.

Examiners' notes

Remember that material on the globalization of migration can be useful for some questions on demography.

Assimilation and multiculturalism

Political controversies regarding migration often involve differences of view over which is preferable: **assimilation** or **multiculturalism**.

Assimilation involves the belief that immigrants should generally take on the culture and characteristics of the population of the country to which they move.

Multiculturalism involves the view that the cultural distinctiveness of an immigrant group should be preserved and celebrated.

Roger Ballard (2002) criticizes policies of assimilation, arguing that any attempt to force immigrant communities to integrate will likely provoke a reaction that makes the divisions wider. In any case, assimilation is generally doomed to failure. From his point of view, it is far better – through positive social policies – to recognize and provide for the diversity of cultures in a country.

Radical critics of multiculturalism, such as Donald and Rattansi (1992), argue that it distracts attention from the real underlying causes of the tensions caused by immigration: the exploitation, discrimination and inequality that are suffered by many immigrant groups.

Globalization and the family

As well as affecting migration, globalization can also have a number of impacts on families and personal life. Deborah Chambers (2012) identifies the following effects:

- More mothers from less developed countries are separating from children and other family members as they seek work in more developed countries to support their families financially. New technology (e.g. Skype) may allow continued contact, but both mothers and children (and other family members) can find the separation traumatic.
- Chambers uses Hochschild's idea (2003) of **global chains of care** to discuss how career-orientated Western women come to rely on migrant workers to carry out caring tasks for their families, while leaving a **care gap** for the families of the migrants.
- There is a tendency for migrants to marry within their cultural group in order to maintain cultural traditions.
- There is an increase in internet dating and 'mail-order brides' as Western men seek younger partners and women from poorer countries seek lives in the West. However, Chambers believes there is mounting evidence that some women who follow this path suffer abuse.

According to Vanessa May (2015) the sort of trends described above have led to an increase in transnational families, where family members live in different countries. She sees this as partly resulting from global economic changes that have impoverished some people in less developed countries, while economic growth in some developed countries has increased opportunities for migration.

Essential notes

The controversy over migration in the UK's Brexit vote suggests that, as a result of immigration, the politicization of migration takes the form of fear over job loss and wage reduction. However, economists suggest that wage reduction as a result of migration may affect only a small number of workers and that immigration creates new job opportunities, meeting the needs of immigrants as well as increasing the supply of labour.

Examiners' notes

These arguments can be useful in answering a wide range of questions on changes in family life and relationships, e.g. relationships between parents and children.

Changes in the age structure

The age structure refers to the proportion of people in different age groups in a particular population. This can be represented in **population pyramids** (such as fig 15) which divide different segments of the population into age groups and by doing so illustrate the relative proportions of different age groups for these segments.

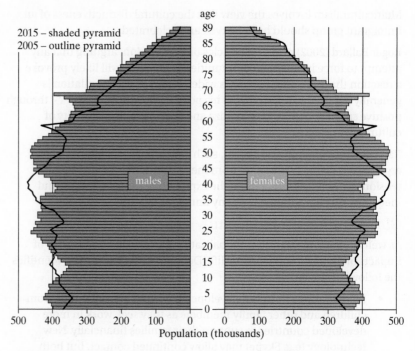

Fig 15
Population estimates UK – mid-2015

Traditionally, population pyramids tend to be triangular, narrowing in older age groups, but recent trends in the UK have produced an **ageing population** with a rising proportion of elderly and middle aged people and a falling proportion, which of children and younger adults. For example, the average age of people in the UK was 40 in 2013 but just 34 in 1971.

From 2005 to 2015 the number of males aged over 85 increased by more than 50% and the number of females in the same age group by more than 20%. On projected trends, by 2034, 23% of the population will be over 65, while just 18% will be under 16.

The **median** age (the age of the person in the middle of the age distribution) increased from 35 years in 1984 to 40 in 2015 and is projected to rise further.

Reasons for the ageing population

The main reasons for an ageing population are:

- The falling death rate – people tend to survive more years after reaching adulthood, leading to more elderly in the population.
- The falling birth rate and fertility rate – children constitute a proportion of the population.

The effects of an ageing population

An ageing population can have a number of effects.

The dependency ratio

The rising proportion of the population beyond retirement age increases the economic burden on those of working age who need to pay taxes to cover the costs associated with the retired population, such as pensions and healthcare.

Effects on families

An ageing population can place extra economic, emotional and practical burdens on adults of working age who may need to care for elderly parents as well as raising children. This burden tends to fall particularly heavily on women, who usually end up being the main carers.

Government spending

Provision for the welfare of the elderly and those over pension age imposes a large burden upon the government. Relatively little in taxes is received from people who are retired but their demands on healthcare are likely to be greater than younger members of the population. In response to this problem the government in the UK has restricted the amount of support provided for care of the elderly and has started to raise retirement ages. Under the current plans, the state pension age will rise from 60 to 66 for women and from 65 to 66 for men by 2020. Between 2024 and 2046 the state pension will rise further to 68 for both men and women.

Social problems for older people

An ageing population will result in increasing numbers of households consisting of single pensioners (most often women) living alone. As pension provision is reduced and people live longer the number of retired people living in poverty is likely to increase.

However, these problems should not be exaggerated since the health of older groups in the population has been improving, making it possible for more people to remain economically active longer and placing less burden on health and social services.

Perspectives on old age

The functionalists Elena Cumming and William Henry (1961) see the **disengagement** of older people from society as beneficial. (Disengagement involves gradual withrawal from social roles.) If older people continue working, for example, they will block opportunities for younger people and they may become less competent in performing their roles in society.

Hockey and James (1993) argue that old age is a social construction and that many people above retirement age are capable of carrying out a wide range of social roles if society did not expect, and sometimes require, them to withdraw from those roles, for example to retire from work.

Examiners' notes

It is important to emphasize in answers that an ageing population can be the result of low birth and fertility rates just as much as it can be a result of increasing life expectancy.

Essential notes

See pages 60–63 and 64–65 for information covering the reasons for the falling birth rate and the falling death rate.

Essential notes

It is useful to make a link to feminism here: a number of feminists have studied the ways in which the care of elderly parents restricts the life chances of women.

Examiners' notes

The examiner will be impressed if you get some balance into your answer by showing that there are some positive aspects to the ageing population such as improvement in health.

Chapter 7: General tips for AS Families and Households Paper 2

The AQA Families and Households exam questions are part of Paper 2 (7191) and there are five compulsory questions to answer – all in Section B of the exam. The maximum number of marks you can achieve for this section is 40 (divided between the questions as shown below – 2:2:6:10:20). You are allowed an hour and a half (90 minutes) for Paper 2. Spend at least 55 minutes on the Families and Households questions, and also allow 5 minutes to read the item that will help you to answer the 20-mark question. The item is a guide to help you think about the question, but do not just recycle it. Short-answer questions 8, 9 and 10 should be answered in a clear and concise manner. Don't spend too much time on these – that way, you have longer for the questions with more marks. The longer questions, 11 and 12, should be written in continuous prose and you will be assessed on the use of good English and appropriate sociological terms, as well as your organization.

The following explanations give more detail about what you should expect from each question on Paper 2 and some guidance on how to achieve high marks.

- **Question 8** is worth **2 marks** and it will ask you **to define** a term. Although this answer does not need to be long, you must not bullet point your answer. To get the full 2 marks, you must define the term fully, explaining any element that includes key terms. Avoid repeating the term, and explain all parts of it. For example, if asked to define serial monogamy, you would get 1 mark for a partial definition such as 'Serial monogamy refers to having a series of partners', and the second mark for adding 'but not at the same time'. A single sentence will be enough to be awarded full marks.

  Always have a go at defining the term in the question; think about your knowledge and link it back to a topic that you have studied within Families and Households. There is a good chance you may be awarded a mark even if you are not sure about the term, so it is worth a try. See the glossary at the back of this book, which contains some key words. It is really good exam practice to have a go at defining these.

- **Question 9** is worth **2 marks**. It will ask you **to explain** briefly a concept or trend using just one example. Although this is a short-answer question, you need to explain your example fully to achieve the full 2 marks. For example, if the question asks you for a reason why there has been a decline in birth rate, you could write: 'There has been a decline in the birth rate because women have more choice' [1 mark], then 'This means that they do not have as many children as they used to; smaller families have become more preferable' [1 mark].

  This question is more complex than the other 2-mark question and it is advised that you use two sentences. You will most likely need to write an identifier (the reason) and a qualifier (the explanation) to achieve the full 2 marks. Keep an eye on timing, as the question is worth 2 marks and you should avoid spending too long on this – 3 minutes maximum.

- **Question 10** is worth **6 marks**. It will ask you for **three reasons** for a social happening. Again, you must fully explain the reason to get the full 6 marks. One mark is awarded for each identifier, and another mark for the development or qualifier of each identifier. You might be asked for three reasons why women are delaying childbirth. One identifier could be contraception [1 mark] – women have easier access to it now – and much more choice [1 mark]. Another reason is because of careers [1 mark] – women want to have a career before they have children, meaning they have them later in life [1 mark]. A final reason is that there is less social stigma [1 mark] – it is much more common now for women to have children later in life [1 mark].

  Be very clear that you have provided three answers. Use the identifiers 1, 2, 3 if it helps, or write three separate sentences. Perhaps put them on different lines. You can give more than three reasons – the examiner will mark all of your reasons and credit the best ones.

- **Question 11** is worth **10 marks**. Essentially you will select **two examples** of something and apply it to an area of Families and Households. Any question awarded 10 marks or more must be written in continuous prose and you will be examined on good use of English, organizational structure and use of sociological vocabulary. As you use two examples, you will need to develop each idea in some depth to achieve full marks. The 10 marks are awarded for the overall quality of both examples together, rather than 5 marks per example. This question is marked in bands, 8–10, 7–9, 4–6, 1–3 and 0. To get into the top bracket, make sure you have clearly identified your two examples and have fully explained them with some examples and analysis. Also draw a conclusion about which example is stronger or has more of an impact.

It is essential that you remember the need for analysis in this answer and ensure you develop your points much more fully than in the first three questions (questions 8–10). Think of it as a mini essay, with two separate parts and perhaps a very short conclusion. Remember: about 15 minutes is allocated to this question, so the amount you write should reflect this.

- **Question 12** is an essay that carries **20 marks**, and you will be spending around 30 minutes on it. You will be asked to apply the material in the item, plus your wider sociological knowledge. Therefore you must use the item as a guide and develop the ideas within it. You must also include relevant material that is not present in the item. To get top marks, your answer must demonstrate that you have detailed knowledge and you should present a range of points that have depth. You must select appropriate and relevant material to help you answer the question. Make sure you include some analysis and evaluation; for example, you may decide to compare ideas from other sociological perspectives. Like other longer questions, this question is marked using mark-bands, and you should aim to reach as high as you can within the highest mark-bands. For the top mark-band (17–20), you will be expected to give a short introduction to the topic, provide detailed knowledge and show strong understanding, with the use of plenty of concepts. You will also have to apply your material well to the question, and have clear and explicit evaluation of the strengths and weaknesses of different arguments, leading to a conclusion.

For example, if the question asks you to assess the contribution of Marxism to our understanding of the family, you could select three Marxists to analyse: Engels, Zaretsky and Althusser. For each one, explain any ideas or concepts and expand on their views of the family. You could support this with examples from family life. You could then evaluate each theorist using other sociological theories, such as feminism and functionalism. As a minimum you will need to explain the view in the question, look at theories and/ or evidence and/or arguments to support this view, do the same with views, theories, arguments and evidence that do not support the statement, and reach a conclusion about the strengths of the arguments of the two sides.

When writing essays you should look back regularly to the question – this helps you to focus on the set question. Make sure you have obeyed all of the instructions and covered all of the issues included in the question. Some essays have two or more parts. You will only gain top marks if you deal with each part. Do not be tempted to write an essay about all you know on the topic in question, or to spend time writing at a tangent to the question – use your material to focus on the issues. This is challenging, especially if you are unsure of the view in the question. Therefore, rather than presenting everything you know, just keep reading the item. Make some notes on your question paper to see if you can draw out knowledge that is more relevant to the question.

Families and Households (sample AS exam Paper 2)

Questions

08 Define the term 'joint conjugal roles'. [**2 marks**]

09 Using **one** example, briefly explain why there have been changes to the birth rate. [**2 marks**]

10 Outline **three** reasons for the decline in marriage rates in the UK. [**6 marks**]

11 Outline **two** ways in which the changes in social policy have affected family diversity. [**10 marks**]

12 Read **Item A** and answer the question that follows.

Item A

Feminist sociologists show concern over family life for women. They argue that woman face an unequal balance of domestic labour, which can sometimes be added to by paid external work. Some of the work women conduct is invisible and is impossible to measure. The family also has a 'dark side' and women may be exploited by unequal power relationships. Other sociologists argue that family life has improved greatly for women.

Applying material from **Item A** and your own knowledge, evaluate the contribution of feminist views to our understanding of the family.

[**20 marks**]

Grade C answers

08 *Define the term 'joint conjugal roles'.* [**2 marks**]

> 'Joint conjugal roles' is the term used to describe what household tasks a couple performs in relation to the division of domestic labour. 'Joint' means that domestic tasks are shared between the two.

This answer clearly displays a sound understanding of conjugal roles. The student has identified that it is a term used to describe how the division of labour is carried out. So the first part of this answer scores 1 mark. The student then achieves the second mark by stating that 'joint' means the male and female share tasks in the household.
Mark: 2/2

---

09 *Using **one** example, briefly explain why there have been changes to the birth rate.* [**2 marks**]

> There have been changes in the birth rate because family sizes have become smaller.

This answer clearly states that there has been a decrease in the birth rate – this explains a trend or pattern linked to the birth rate and scores 1 mark. The further mark could have been achieved by developing the idea, stating that families only have one or two children, or that it is because children are an economic liability and therefore couples don't have many. **Mark: 1/2**

10 *Outline **three** reasons for the decline in marriage rates in the UK.* [**6 marks**]

> One reason for the decline in marriage is secularization. Marriage is attached to many religions. People are no longer religious and therefore do not engage in marriage. A second reason marriage rates are in decline is because of cost. A final reason for the decline in marriage rates is choice and no stigma.

11 *Outline **two** ways in which the changes in social policy have affected family diversity.* [**10 marks**]

> One way the changes in social policy have affected family diversity is the Civil Partnership Act in 2004. This allowed same-sex couples to have a civil union or marriage. This has changed further since then, which means same-sex couples can now have a proper wedding and are given the same legal rights as heterosexual couples. This means that there will be a rise in same-sex couples and same-sex families. The change in law made this legal, which means it is socially acceptable. Another way in which policy impacts family diversity is the Divorce Reform Act 1969. This brought in the concept of irretrievable breakdown and made it easier to get divorced. A couple no longer needed to prove guilt or blame and could get divorced if they felt that their marriage was at a natural end. This was also amended in 1984, which means couples can now file divorce after just one year of marriage. This has meant a rise in the number of single parent families. 90% of all single parent families are headed by women.

This candidate shows three clear reasons, which are presented in a way that is easy to see. For example, the first reason is secularization, which scores 1 mark; this is then further developed to state that it is a loss of religion and marriage is a religious act. The second reason is cost, which scores 1, but the student misses an opportunity to gain the second mark by developing the idea. The candidate could have developed the idea that, especially if weddings are lavish, they can cost large sums of money. The final reason actually displays two credit-worthy points: choice and stigma. To gain the second mark the candidate could have developed either of those identifiers, by exploring the notion of choice or describing how stigma has changed. **Mark: 4/6**

This candidate shows a clear understanding of social policy. Two examples are selected that are explicitly linked to family diversity: civil partnership and the increase of same sex families, and divorce reforms and the increase of lone parent families. The first way scores highly, as the answer accurately explains the change in legal rights for same-sex couples and also provides the correct year of the act. There is a lack of further analysis here, which could have scored more marks. For example, the candidate could have stated that many same-sex couples are having children. Postmodernism could have also been used to support the idea of change and choice. The second reason, again, is clearly identified as social policy on divorce. The student selects the correct policy and year and expands, showing more knowledge by stating that the Divorce Reform Act was also amended. The candidate knows that more divorces means more single parent families. The candidate could move into the next bracket by adding a deeper level of analysis with the use of theory and adding a short conclusion to reach the top band. Both reasons are valid and conceptually detailed and even. The answer is written in continuous prose and has a good use of English and specialist terminology.
Mark: 6/10

This candidate displays a good base knowledge of feminism. There is use of specialized terminology to explain the key concerns of feminism. The candidate could have developed this by stating what the different types of feminism are – this would have displayed wider knowledge.

The candidate's first use of the item – this must be done in order to achieve good marks. The student clearly highlights here they are drawing material from the item.

Correctly identified knowledge and understanding.

Good use of sociological concept.

The candidate can also compare this to men.

Here the candidate evaluates for the first time. This is a developed evaluative point, as theory is correctly used. This could have been developed to explain why functionalists believe this to be so.

Knowledge and understanding is being displayed. The candidate also develops the study and clearly has good understanding of it.

Again the candidate uses the item correctly and develops the ideas within. The candidate could develop the idea of emotion work further.

Here is a basic evaluation that is evaluated with depth. Theory is used, which is then developed further with Marxist feminism – there is some evaluation here.

12 *Applying material from* **Item A** *and your own knowledge, evaluate the contribution of feminist views to our understanding of the family.*
   [20 marks]

Feminism is a conflict theory which presents the nature of patriarchy as being at the heart of the conflict. Feminists suggest that women face inequality in all spheres of life including the family. There are different types of feminism. They all believe in slightly different things but share the idea that every aspect of society is patriarchal. All of them have written about the family.

The item suggests that women do more work in the family which is known as the domestic division of labour. Feminists have been fascinated with this area of sociology because they believe that is in the family where women face most inequality. Dunscumbe and Marsden argue that women face a dual burden, they do all of the housework and child care but they also have to work in paid employment also. Men on the other hand do not do much housework, if any and just have paid employment. Since women have entered the workforce it means more women have to juggle the dual burden. Functionalists such as Parsons are critical of this as they suggest that women are naturally suited to the housework.

Ann Oakley who is a feminist, did a study on housework and found that women are responsible for the majority of household chores and childcare. She also found that every hour women spend on housework is equal for 10 minutes for a man. This clearly shows that women are doing far more than men in the family. Furthermore the family exploits women in terms of the work they do, as stated in the item some of the work carried out by women is invisible. The mother of the family is seen to take on a nurturing role and makes sure that all of the members in the family are happy. There is no ways of measuring how long women are spending on this type of work. It is a strength that feminists have highlighted this type of strain. Functionalists are critical of this view and see it being the woman's job to perform such tasks. Parsons argues that women play an expressive role and are suited to emotional work. Margaret Benston a Marxist feminist would disagree with this. The work that women do in the family is devalued and unpaid.

Feminists highlight not only the inequality in the domestic division of labour, but also the nature of patriarchal power relationships in the family. Edgell looked into the decision Making process in the family. Leighton who is a feminist discovered that when the man is unemployed the power does transfer to the female in the family which shows things may be changing. Pahl also looked at money in the family and found that it is mainly men who control the money in the household. However it is worth noting that this concept could be outdated many women now go to work and some are even the main bread winners.

Accurate knowledge. This answer is now starting to display a wide range of knowledge. This paragraph has three sociologists in it, clearly displaying knowledge is wide-ranging. However, it lacks depth. There is a basic attempt at evaluation.

The item also suggests that the family has a dark side to it. The work of feminists has helped to highlight the fact that women can be exploited in the worst way in the family and suffer from abuse. Dobash and Dobash estimate that one in four women will become a victim of domestic violence in their lifetime. Two women a week will die as a result of a violent partner in the UK and that most violence takes place in between the hours of 9pm and 3am. This is truly shocking and disturbing without the work of feminists we would not have an insight into these statistics. Also more men are becoming victims of domestic violence. Because if the work of such feminists laws have been changed for example in 1991 the rape amendment act made rape within marriage illegal.

It is clear to see that the work of feminists have helped us to understand that family life can be patriarchal and that women are disadvantaged in terms of house work, yet it is worth noting that things are changing.

This is the third time the candidate has used the item and developed the issues raised, clearly showing the student had a good understanding of the topic area.

Here is a link to social policy, which shows very good depth of knowledge. **[Mark: 14/20]**

Total marks: 2 + 1 + 4 + 6 + 14 = 27/40 = Grade C

More sample questions

08 Define the term 'household'. **[2 marks]**
09 Using **one** example, briefly explain why Britain has an ageing population. **[2 marks]**
10 Outline **three** reasons which may pull individuals to migrate to the UK. **[6 marks]**
11 Identify and explain **two** reasons why family diversity may have increased. **[10 marks]**
12 Read **Item A** and answer the question that follows.

> **Item A**
> Postmodernists argue that the family has undergone many changes. The nuclear family would have once been the most dominant family type in the UK. However there are many other family types in the UK, people have more choice in what type of family they live in. Other family types are now more acceptable.

Applying material from **Item A** and your own knowledge, evaluate the view that there is no longer one dominant family type in the UK.

[20 marks]

The final part of this answer continues on the next two pages

General tips for A level Families and Households Paper 2

The AQA Topics in Sociology exam (7192/2) consists of eight topics in total. Section A is the first compulsory section, where you will find four topics. Answer the topic you have studied.

The second section of the exam paper, also compulsory, is called Section B. You must answer one section from a further four topics. You will find the Families and Households questions in topic A2 of the exam question paper. You have 2 hours (120 minutes) for this paper; therefore you can allow 1 hour (60 minutes) per topic. There are three exam questions to answer for Families and Households, worth a total of 40 marks (divided 10:10:20). You must allow some time to read the items in the Families and Households section. The items are a guide to help you think about the question, but should not just be recycled. However, you must reference them if the item asks you to – for example, the question might ask you to apply your knowledge from Item A and elsewhere.

- **Question 04** will ask you **to outline** two things: for example, two ways in which government policy has affected family life; two different types of family diversity; two demographic trends; two ways in which the position of children has changed, or two reasons why relationships are more equal in the family. These questions are worth **10 marks**.

  To answer these questions, you need to identify two clear ways. Allow yourself 15 minutes to do so – this means your answer will be reasonably developed. The discussion could focus on issues such as why they are significant and how significant they are. To get into the top mark-band (8–10) you will need good knowledge and understanding, to apply it clearly and to include analysis and evaluation. It may be worthwhile including a one- or two-sentence conclusion that links your two points and evaluates how important each of them is.

- **Question 05** is a **10-mark** question, but it is different from the 10-mark question above. This question has an Item attached to it (Item A), and the skill of application is particularly important because you are asked **to apply** the material from the item and analyse two things (e.g. factors, effects, reasons or even changes). For example, you could be asked to analyse two factors that lead to family diversity, or two changes in patterns of marriage and divorce.

  To answer these questions, you will have to identify two points from the item provided that are relevant to the question, and then analyse them. The item will guide you, and it will help shape your ideas, but it must not simply be recycled. The discussion could focus on issues, such as why they are significant and how significant they are, or perhaps what impact they have had on sociology or society. To get into the top mark-band (8–10), you will need good knowledge and understanding, and be able to apply it clearly and include analysis and evaluation. It may be worthwhile including a one- or two-sentence conclusion that links your two points and evaluates how important each of them is. Marks are awarded for the overall quality of both examples together, rather than 5 marks per example.

- **Question 06** is an essay question worth **20 marks**, so this is the most valuable question on the paper, and should take up around 30 minutes of your time. It takes the same form as the 20-mark AS question. However, as you have extra time to answer it and an item to read to help your ideas, you will need more depth and detail in your knowledge and understanding, and be able to apply these consistently to the question across your whole answer and to further develop your analysis and evaluation. Compared with 10-mark questions, you will have more time to explore contradictory arguments and to discuss all sides of a debate more fully. You will be expected to feature sociological theory in your answer to this question. It will ask you **to apply** material from Item B and to use your own knowledge to evaluate a viewpoint. It will therefore be based upon an area of the sociology within Families and Households in the specification where there are differences of view. For example, it might ask you to compare one theory of the family with another, or to assess the roles of men and women in the family.

  This question, like other longer questions, is marked using mark-bands, and your aim should be to get as high up as you can in the highest mark-bands you can get into. The top mark-band gains you 17–20 marks, for which you will be expected to show detailed knowledge and a strong understanding, with the use of plenty of concepts. You will also have to apply your material well to the question, and have clear and explicit evaluation of the strengths and weaknesses of different arguments, leading to a conclusion. As a minimum, you will need to explain the view in the question, look at theories and/or evidence and/or arguments to support this view, do the same with views, theories, arguments and evidence that do not support the statement, and reach a conclusion about the strengths of the arguments of the two sides. The question is supported by the use of an item, which you must refer to. This shows the examiner you have read and understood the implications of it. You may want to refer to the item early on in your essay, as the ideas within it may help shape and structure your writing. To make sure that the material you select meets the demands of the question, you may find it useful to refer back to the question at several stages – this will also help you to stay on track and on topic.

Families and Households (sample A level exam Paper 2)

*This candidate would be placed in the 4–7 band. You can see that the candidate has the knowledge. They have been able to provide two clear and concise reasons. The reason this response would score no higher is because it lacks depth. For example, the candidate discusses extended families yet they could have gone on to state the type of extended family. They also use Brannen for the relevant sociologists, but then they fail to analyse what Brannen actually discovered about extended families. The second reason again shows good sociological knowledge. The candidate has used the appropriate sociological terminology by the discussion of matrifocal families. There is basic analysis. **Mark: 5/10***

This answer clearly displays two different reasons for the change in position of women and it is places in the 4–7 band. The answer shows good sociological knowledge but it does remain underdeveloped with little analysis. For example, the candidate correctly identifies that feminists support women in the workforce, but there is no further development of this. The candidate could have linked in a type of feminism, or social policy. In the second point the student discusses conjugal roles but they never really analyse the idea. They could have described

Questions

04 Outline two ways in which increased migration to the UK has affected family structure. **[10 marks]**

05 Read **Item A** below and answer the question that follows.

> ### Item A
>
> The 1950s was seen as the golden era of family life by some sociologists. Women played an expressive role which meant they were confined to the home. The main responsibility of the female in the family was to look after the children and make sure all of the household chores were done. Women spent hours cooking, cleaning, and washing while men went out to work and were the head of the household.

Applying material from **Item A**, analyse two changes in the position of women in society over the last 100 years. **[10 marks]**

06 Read **Item B** below and answer the question that follows.

> ### Item B
>
> Functionalist sociologists share the view that the traditional nuclear family provides functions which are necessary for the smooth running of society. Without the nuclear family children would not receive adequate socialization. Children need both a male and female figure to look up to and imitate. This helps children learn gender roles. The nuclear family is the most effective type of family to make sure children are brought up in a stable loving environment.

Applying the material from **Item B** and your knowledge, evaluate the view that the nuclear family is the best fit for the smooth running of society today. **[20 marks]**

Grade C answers

04 *Outline two ways in which increased migration to the UK has affected family structure.* **[10 marks]**

One way increased migration has affected family structure is more extended families. When Asians come to the UK they usually bring grandparents with them. They all live together in the same house in one big family. The younger members can look after the older members. Brannen is the sociologist for this.

Another way in which increased migration has affected family life is black matrifocal families. Afro Caribbean women tend to live in single parent families. The father is not involved and many women rely on extended family support. These families are headed by strong women who are able to raise their children alone without a man.

05 *Applying material from **Item A,** analyse two changes in the position of women in society over the last 100 years.* [**10 marks**]

One change in the position of women is that they are no longer in the housewife role. Many women now go out to work and do really important jobs. Feminists think this is a good thing. Year ago this would not have been possible for women as it was an expectation that they would stay at home and do all of the housework. In modern society this expectation has changed and it's OK for women to go out to work. They can do this and have a family.

A second change in the position of women is that men now also do the housework too. This is called joint conjugal roles. 50 years ago there would have been separate roles and that's when women did do all of the housework but now it's more joint.

06 *Applying the material from **Item B** and your knowledge, evaluate the view that the nuclear family is the best fit for the smooth running of society today.* [**20 marks**]

The theory in the item is functionalism. Functionalists think that the nuclear family is the best family type for the UK. There are many reasons why functionalists think this but other sociologists don't always agree.

One reason why functionalists think the nuclear family is best is because it is best for socializing young children. This is Parsons. Parsons says that the nuclear family has a mum and a dad. This is the best for families because the children can learn their gender roles. Little boys can watch their fathers and help them with the DIY. Little girls can watch their mothers and help them with cooking and cleaning, so the children know what is expected of them when they get older. Not all sociologists agree with this. For example feminists think that this needs to change as little girls need to aspire more and not just watch their mums do housework.

Murdock who is a functionalist suggests that the family performs some other important functions too. They are the education of children, which is similar to Parsons. The sexual function, the reproductive function and the economic function. For example the reproductive function, this is needed for people to have children. It is best to have children in a stable loving family. This is good way to bring children into the world they will have both a mother a father and this is very stable. It is worth noting though that some people do not plan to break up or separate it might not be their fault. Another function is the economic function. This links to society in general, it costs money to have children. It costs money to raise children. If there are two parents the chances are that they can cope with the money needed to have kids. They will get a bit of money off the government but they won't need any more help. So this is good for society. The new right theory like this as they think that people get too many benefits like single mums. These benefits would not be needed if there was two parents in as nuclear family.

what conjugal roles are, and attached a sociologist to support, or link to, sociological theory. The answer is clear and concise, yet underdeveloped. **Mark: 5/10**

The student has used the item.

Although the candidate makes a valid point, it is vague. Also the student recognizes that theories support the functionalist ideology, but they could have displayed more knowledge and analysis by stating which theories.

The student identifies a function of the family and links it to Parsons. However, there is a lack of depth on Parsons' ideas. There could be a discussion of his two irreducible functions.

This knowledge is accurate, but it is basic and lacks depth.

The candidate makes the first evaluative statement in the essay. It is basic and lacks development, but it does use theory. The candidate could have suggested which feminists are critical of this, with a deeper discussion of gender role socialization.

The candidate is displaying knowledge and correctly identifies all of Murdock's functions.

The candidate misses an opportunity here to discuss family demographics

This is a basic evaluative statement. The candidate is recognizing that the nuclear family is a shared life goal but not possible for all people due to unforeseen circumstances. This is quite a sophisticated idea.

The candidate makes a good link to social policy, but it could be further developed by naming the benefit given and its impact on child-rearing.

The candidate attempts evaluation accurately again, and links it to the correct sociological theory. It could be developed by the addition of the thoughts of Charles Murray.

The student links back to the question here, which shows a good level of understanding.

The student offers a reasoned conclusion, but does miss an opportunity to discuss family diversity. **[Mark: 13/20]**

The functionalist idea of the nuclear family being the best for society does work. The family does spend time teaching children the norms and values that they will need for the future. But it is an out dated view. Not all families are nuclear anymore, that doesn't mean they can't perform the functions it just means it might be done in different ways.

This answer just makes it into the 13–16 bracket, but it does stay at the bottom. This is because it does show a reasonable range of knowledge. There are two target theory aspect points: discussion of Parsons and Murdock. The knowledge is less developed in places, which is why it goes no further into the band. Application is largely explicit, although opportunities are missed to develop this. Appropriate analysis is there but does lack depth. There is some evaluation, with a use of two other sociological theories. Opportunities are missed to develop this further.

Total marks: 5 + 5 + 13 = 23/40 = Grade C

Grade A answers

04 *Outline two ways in which increased migration to the UK has affected family structure.* **[10 marks]**

Although this answer does not give equal weighting for each point, it still gets into the top mark-band. This candidate clearly identifies two ways in which increased migration has affected family life. Both of the suggestions given by the candidate display good knowledge and understanding, which is required for this band. Both applications are developed, with the first showing a sophisticated analysis of the effect on family structure. The candidate accurately uses two different sociologists in the first application. Although no sociologists are used in the second application, sociological theory has been used and applied. The candidate also concludes by stating that migration does affect family structure, but despite this the family is changing. **Mark: 8/10**

One way that an increase in migration can affect family structure in the UK is the growth of extended families. Rapoport and Rapoport suggested that the family does have organisational diversity. When south Asian migrants moved to the UK it became important to keep the whole family together and therefore other family members may have also migrated to the UK. If this takes the form of older generations it is known as vertically extended. Many south Asians live in vertically extended families as looking after older members of the family is important. Bhatti noted that Asian families do have different family structures, norms and values which are stricter and old fashioned. The concept of 'izzat' or honour is passed down, especially by the elders of the family. We have also noted a growth in the number of horizontally extended families. According to the Rapoports, this type of diversity is where other family members live together such as Aunts, Uncles and cousins. We can also see this type of diversity in the UK. In Asian households other families may also migrate and live in the same house, as they may be helping out with businesses, or gaining an education and therefore it makes good sense to share accommodation.

Another way that immigration can affect family structure in the UK is the rise of multi-cultural families. Postmodernists suggest that we are living in a hybrid world where identity is become more mixed and people have more choice. The level of diversity in the UK has increased with the people who migrate here. It is only natural that people will fall in love, and there is no social stigma attached to multi-cultural marriage like there used to be. This means that we will see a rise in the number of multi-cultural hybrid families. Family structure will continue to change in the UK as we are postmodern. This could be down to migration or simply down to social change.

05 *Applying material from **Item A**, analyse two changes in the position of women in society over the last 100 years.* [**10 marks**]

Item A describes the life of women when gender roles were more traditional. Talcott Parsons suggests that women were suited to the expressive role of house work and childcare, while men were suited to the instrumental role, working and being the breadwinner. This notion is now outdated as the position of women has changed. Women are no longer confined by the expressive role and have been entering the work place at a fast rate. Some women have even taken over the instrumental role, as many women are now the head of the house hold and the main or sole bread winners. Liberal feminists argue that changes in the law have aided women on this journey such as the equal pay act and the sex discrimination act.

The position of women has also changed within the division of domestic labour also. Elizabeth Bott suggested two different types of the division of domestic labour. There are separate roles. This features in item A as the female is doing the housework and the men are going out to work. There are also joint conjugal roles which is where the division of domestic labour is more equal. This has changed women's position in the household as they have more power. Wilmott and Young made the suggestion that the family had become more 'symmetrical' with men and women completing a similar amount of domestic chores. Hatter et al also suggests more emphasis is placed on fatherhood. Men are expected to also perform the expressive caring role. This means that emotional work is also shared. This shift in sharing gives women more power in the family proving that their potions have changed, and improved.

Despite the shift and change of position of women in the family feminists are still concerned that some families are still very traditional and exert patriarchal control over women.

This answer achieves full marks because it displays a wide range of knowledge and it is conceptually detailed. Two reasons are applied – both show sound knowledge and understanding and are explicitly linked back to the item. The candidate also analyses theory. The end of the answer displays a good level of evaluation. What more could be expected of the notional 17-/18-year-old?
Mark: 10/10

06 *Applying the material from **Item B** and your knowledge, evaluate the view that the nuclear family is the best fit for the smooth running of society today.* [**20 marks**]

Item B contains in it a description of the Functionalist perspective of the family. Functionalism is a structural concerns theory which works on the basis of the organic analogy. Each institution in society has a role to play in order for society to run smoothly. The family is a very important institution to functionalists, as it is needed for the smooth running of society. Hence why the item suggests the nuclear family is the best fit for society. It is worth noting that the nuclear family is a functionalist term and refers to a heterosexual married couple. Who have a small number of children. While functionalists idealize this type of family, other family types do exist.

One of the earliest functionalist writers on the 'nuclear' family was George Murdock. Murdock studies over 250 societies and claimed the nuclear family

This an excellent introduction. The candidate references the item and explicitly links it to the material. The candidate also displays knowledge of the functionalist perspective and defines the term 'nuclear' family. Knowledge is developed by stating that there are other family types. This indicates there will be analysis of this later on in the essay.

The correct sociologist is selected for the topic and a good base range of knowledge is displayed.

was most predominant. Murdock suggested that the family performed four functions to aid the smooth running of society. The first function was the sexual function. By this he meant that sexual behaviour is best contained in a loving marital relationship. You can see that this would be an overly romantic view, but it would lesson unplanned pregnancy and lower sexually transmitted infections, it makes sense. However feminists have criticized this is it has always been seen as a woman's duty to have sex with her husband. Women in a difficult positions. This was reflected in law, the rape amendment act in 1991 made rape within marriage illegal. Although feminists support this act, the fact it come in the 90s shows how this was an old ideology that needed to change. The second function is that of education. Children need to be taught essential norms and values in order to fit into society. For example the value of family is taught and nuclear ideology can be passed on. Other norms and values can be taught like manners and education. That was children can learn the value consensus and society and continue smoothly. The third function was reproductive. People need to have children for the continuation of the population, surely the best way to do this is in a safe enviroment where children have two parents to look after them? This is a stable way to reproduce. Marxists such as Engels have been critical of this as they see the nuclear family as a way for the bourgeoisie to maintain their wealth. They need to be sure of their heirs so they pass it on and the wealth stays in the family. The final function is the economic function. Two parents male and female are the most economical way to have a family. The male can go to work and provide all of the income for family. While the female can stay at home and look after the children do the housework. This means the family is a self-sufficient unit needing no help from welfare state. Every family receives child benefit, although the conservative government has just made it means tested. The amount is around 20 pounds a week of the first child, this is minimal compared to families that need more support such as single parent families. The new right theory supports this idea. Charles Murray suggests a generous welfare state creates welfare dependency and offers perverse incentives for single mothers.

Talcott Parsons another functionalist disagreed with Murdock as he suggested the family has two irreducible functions. The socialisation of children and the stabilisation of adult personalities. Parsons argued that children need a parent of either gender in order to learn their gender role. They can then learn through role imitation and encouragement what is appropriate for their gender. Feminists are highly critical of this. Ann Oakley suggests children are manipulated and canalized into their gender role. Unless this practise changes there will always be inequality and patriarchy. The second function according to Parsons is the stabilization of adult personalities otherwise known as the warm bath theory. The female must carry out her gender role in order to hold the family together. Again feminists are critical of this as it puts the female in a subordinate positions. Also she soaks up the frustrations of her husband putting her in a vulnerable position. Dobash and Dobash suggest that 1 in 5 women will be a victim of domestic violence in their life. This is a very serious issue, one which functionalists ignore.

Finally the nuclear family may perform many functions but that does not mean that other family types cannot perform the same things. The nuclear family is an outdated idea. Divorce rates at an all-time high. Postmodernists suggest

---

This candidate has made a developed evaluative statement, displaying a good level of sophistication, linking the point to social policy and law change.

Again the candidate has shown a sophisticated evaluation technique, which is fully supported with the use Marxism.

Another link to social policy displays a greater range of knowledge here. It is clear that this answer is heading for the top band.

The candidate does evaluate here. However, this could be more developed by analysing the New Right/neoliberal theory in more depth.

A second key theorist on the target aspect of the question.

The candidate evaluates with the use of theory and provides a relevant example.

There is a clear link to the question here.

Use of theory to support.

that there is family diversity within Great Britain. There is a growing number of single parent families. Most of these are headed by women. Yet children still learn their gender role despite there is only one parent of one gender. Since the civil partnership act in 2004, there has also been a rise in same sex families. This goes against the idea of the functionalist's nuclear family. But again it does not mean that children are inadequately socialized. Feminists note that the position of women has changed drastically, women no longer do the expressive role and are often the heads of the household. This does not means the family functions any less well than before it just means that it has changed. [18]

It is clear to see that the nuclear family does perform some functions well and it will always be a desired family type in the UK. However the family has undergone many changes and functionalism is outdated.

> Policy is used to support the point.

> Here is the conclusion. Although it is short, it is concise and relates back to the question. [Mark: 18/20]

Total marks: 8 + 10 + 18 = 36/40 = Grade A

More sample questions

04 Outline and briefly explain two reasons for the increase in same-sex couples in the UK. [**10 marks**]

05 Read **Item A** and answer the question that follows.

Item A

Over the years the fertility rate has decreased. Average family size has dropped and it is common for people to have small families. Many years ago couples would have had 6 children. By the 1950s the average was 2.4; however, it is now estimated that average family size stands at around 1.7.

Applying material from **Item A,** outline two reasons for the decline in the fertility rate. [**10 marks**]

06 Read **Item B** and answer the question that follows.

Item B

The position of children in society has changed. Children were once limited in terms of being able to enjoy a childhood and they were given little time to play. Often children would be sent to work from a young age as they were seen as economic assets. This thinking changed and soon policy was put in place to protect children: they were not forced to work and there was a shift in thinking towards a child-centred society.

Applying material from **Item B** and your knowledge, evaluate the view that there has been a march of progress in childhood.

[**20 marks**]

Families and households

Absolute poverty	Lacking the resources to pay for the basic necessities of life such as food, shelter, basic health care and warmth
Achieved status	A position in society which affects the way others view you that is earned at least partly through your own efforts, e.g. a job
Adultist	Biased in favour of the interests or viewpoints of adults at the expense of children
Ageing population	A situation in which an increasing proportion of the population in a given country is middle aged or older
Alienation	A sense of being distanced from something so that it feels alien, e.g. feeling a lack of connection and fulfilment in work
Apollonian image of the child	Sees children as being born good but requiring the good aspects of their nature to be coaxed out of them sympathetically
Ascribed status	A position in society which affects the way others view you that is given by birth, e.g. being male or female
Assimilation	The process by which immigrants become increasingly integrated into a population and change cultural characteristics so they become less distinctive from the non-immigrant population
Beanpole family	A family in which links between generations, i.e. between grandparents, parents and grandchildren, are strong but links with other relations such as aunts, uncles and cousins are weak
Birth rate	The number of live births per thousand of the population per year
Black feminism	A version of **feminism** which argues that racial/**ethnic** differences between women are very important
Bourgeoisie	The **ruling class** in **capitalism** who own property such as capital, businesses and shares
Breadwinner	The person doing all or most of the paid work in order to pay for the expenses of a family
Capitalist society/ capitalism	A society in which people are employed for wages, and businesses are set up with the aim of making a profit
Care gap	A shortage of capacity to care for family members, e.g. the lack of time for working parents to care for their children and the problems produced when mothers from less developed countries emigrate in search of work but leave their children behind
Cereal packet image of the family	The image of the family often presented in marketing as a conventional heterosexual **nuclear family** of legally married couples with one or more (but not too many) children, with a male **breadwinner** and a female housewife
Child-centred	A situation in which the interests of children are put before the interests of adults
Chosen families	Groups of people who are treated like and seen as family members even when they are not related by blood or marriage; friends can be members of chosen families
Chronological age	The number of years since you were born
Civil partnership	A legal partnership of two people, whether homosexual or heterosexual, with similar rights and responsibilities to a marriage
Class/social class	Groups within society distinguished by their economic position and who are therefore unequal, e.g. the middle class in better paid non-manual jobs and the working class in less well-paid physical jobs

Cohabitation/ cohabiting	Living together in an intimate relationship without being married
Competition	When individuals or businesses try to do better than one another, e.g. in selling more goods than another company
Confluent love	Love that is dependent upon partners benefiting from the relationship rather than on unconditional devotion
Conjugal roles	The roles of husband and wife within marriage (it may also be applied to male and female partners who cohabit but are not married)
Death rate	The number of people dying per thousand of the population per year
Deconstruction	The process where something breaks down or is taken apart for the purpose of analysis
De-differentiation	A decline in the importance of differences between things, e.g. a decline in the importance of differences between age groups
Demographic revolution	A situation in which fertility rates and death rates decline as people come to expect lower rates of infant mortality and therefore have fewer children
Dependency ratio	The number of people in non-economically active age groups (children and the retired) relative to the size of the population of working age
Developmentalism	The view that childhood consists of a series of stages in which children develop progressively
Difference feminism	Feminism which emphasizes that the position of women in society varies and women cannot be seen as a single, united group
Dionysian image of the child	Sees children as pursuing their own desires, which can lead to them acting in evil ways
Disengagement	The gradual withdrawal of people from social roles, e.g. older people when they retire
Division of labour	The way in which jobs are divided up between two or more people, e.g. who does which sees them as opposites and believes that children have not yet attained the key characteristics necessary for them to become full persons
Dual-earner families	Families in which both partners are in paid employment
Dysfunctional families	Families which do not function well for family members or in fulfilling social roles, e.g. they fail to socialize children adequately
Economic base	In Marxist theory the foundation of society consisting of the economic system
Economic function	The role the family plays in providing food, shelter and the ability to consume products for its members
Educational function	The role of the family in providing a stable environment in which children can be socialized into the culture of their society
Emotion work	The time and effort involved thinking about and acting to produce the emotional well-being and happiness of others
Empty-shell marriage	A marriage where the partners continue to live together but the emotional attachment and sexual relationship have come to an end
Ethnic group	A group within a population regarded by themselves or by others as culturally distinctive; they usually see themselves as having a common geographic origin

Extended family	The family wider than the nuclear family. As well as parents and children it includes other relatives such as aunts, uncles and grandparents
Extended kinship network	The interrelationships between people related by blood or marriage regardless of whether they live together
Families of choice	Groups of people who have close personal relationships and regard each other as part of their family even if they do not have ties of blood or marriage
Familistic gender regimes	Sets of government policies which support traditional **nuclear families** in which husbands are the main breadwinner and wives do most of the domestic work
Family diversity	The growth of variety in the structure and nature of family types
Female career-core	According to Sheeran, the most basic family unit consisting of a mother and child/children
Female-headed family	Family with a female head of household, usually without an adult male
Feminism	Theory of society which claims that women are disadvantaged and exploited by men, while men are dominant and run society in their own interests
Fertility rate	The number of live births per thousand women aged 15 to 44 per year
Free-market	A system in which businesses can compete with one another without state interference
Friendship networks	Groups of friends who interact with one another without living together
Functionalism	A belief that social institutions serve some positive purpose
Function	A useful job performed by an institution for society
Gay and lesbian households	Households based around male partners or female partners in an intimate, sexual relationship
Gender regimes	Sets of policies which make assumptions about the roles of men and women in family life
Gender roles	The socially expected behaviour of men and women in a particular society
Geographical mobility	The movements of people to different regions or countries
Global chains of care	The interrelationship between **migration** and care when families are split up as a result of migration or other factors
Globalization	The process by which geographical distance and national boundaries become less important as different parts of the world become more interconnected
Heteronorm	The belief that all sexually intimate relationships should be based on heterosexuality
Household	A group of people who share the same accommodation
Identity	The way people are seen by themselves or others in society
Ideological state apparatus	According to Poulantzas, parts of society which encourage people to accept the values favoured by the **ruling class** and which help to maintain **capitalist** society
Ideology	A distorted set of beliefs which favours the interests of a particular social group
Illegitimacy	Children born to unmarried parents
Individualism	An emphasis upon the desires or interests of individual people rather than those of wider social groups
Individualistic gender regimes	Sets of social policies which do not assume that husbands and wives will follow traditional roles and which accommodate the choices made by individuals regardless of whether they are male or female

Individualization	A process in which the wishes of individuals are seen as more important than the maintenance of traditional norms and values, and the prioritization of the interests of individuals above those of social groups
Industrialization	The process whereby manufacturing takes over from agriculture as the most important component in a society's economy
Infant mortality rate	The number of children dying before their first birthday per thousand of live births per year
Intergenerational	Between generations, e.g. between parents and children
Intragenerational	Within a generation, e.g. brothers and sisters
Isolated nuclear family	A **nuclear family** (parents and children) which is relatively self-sufficient and has few contacts with extended kin
Joint conjugal roles	Relationships between husbands and wives in which both do some paid work and both do housework and provide childcare. Typically with this type of role, men and women spend a good deal of time together
Kibbutz	A small communal settlement in Israel
Kin	People linked by blood or marriage
Kinship networks	Interrelationships between people related by blood or marriage whether or not they live together
Late modernity	According to Giddens, the most recent phase in the development of **modernity**
Liberal feminism	A version of **feminism** which is relatively moderate and believes that the position of women in society can be improved through reform rather than radical or revolutionary change
Life course	The development and change in people's lives over periods of time. Unlike life-cycle the life course does not have fixed and predictable stages
Life-cycle	The stages of life, e.g. childhood, young adulthood and old age, which are predictable and assumed to be experienced in the same way by different people
Life expectancy	The average age to which a particular group of people is likely to live
Living apart together	A domestic relationship in which a couple are intimate partners but they do not live in the same household some or all of the time
Lone parent family	Family consisting of one parent living with one or more of their children
Malestream	To **feminists**, something which is mainstream and male-dominated or biased in favour of men
Marital breakdown	The ending of a marriage whether through **divorce**, **separation** or the development of an **empty-shell marriage**
Masculinity	The behaviour and social roles expected of men in a particular culture
Matrifocal family	A family headed by the mother where she is not co-resident with a male partner
Means of production	Those things required to produce goods such as land, machinery, capital, technical knowledge and workers
Median	The middle value in any group, e.g. the median age is the age of the person in a population where half of the people are older than them and half are younger
Media-saturated society	A society in which people's impression of reality is largely shaped by high levels of exposure to the mass media

Metanarrative	A 'big story' about how the world works and how people should live their lives, e.g. a political theory or a religion
Middle class	People who have white-collar jobs which require some qualifications and are generally better paid than **working-class** jobs
Migration	People leaving or entering a country or area to live for a significant time
Modern	Characteristic of or belonging to modernity
Modernity	An era in the development of society characterized by rationality, i.e. planning to achieve goals, and in which the influence of tradition and religion is reduced compared with previous eras
Mode of production	A system of producing things which dominates society, e.g. **capitalism**
Multiculturalism	The policy and practice of celebrating ethnic **diversity** and opposing the idea of **assimilation**
Nayar	Members of a society in southern India
Neo-conventional family	A traditional nuclear family, but one in which both the husband and wife do paid work rather than having a single, male **breadwinner**
Net migration	The difference between the numbers entering and leaving a country (to live for some time rather than just going on holiday)
New reproductive technologies	Technologies which allow previously infertile couples or individuals to have children, e.g. in vitro fertilization (test-tube babies)
New Right	Politicians, thinkers and writers who support the free market rather than state intervention and who believe that traditional moral values should be preserved
Norms	Specific, informal rules of behaviour in a particular society
Nuclear family	A co-resident family of two generations: parents and children
Organizational diversity	Variety in the structure of families, e.g. **lone parent**, **nuclear** and **extended**
Patriarchy/patriarchal	Literally 'rule by the father', usually used by **feminists** to refer to a system in which men have more **power** than women and shape how societies run
Peer group	A group of people with a similar **status** and often age to whom you compare yourself and who may exercise influence on your behaviour
Personal age	How old a person feels rather them how old they actually are
Personal life	The part of your life concerned with relationships with people you are close to, whether friends, family members or lovers
Plastic sexuality	Behaviour where sex can be for pleasure as well as for conceiving children
Pluralization of lifestyles	A process in which people come to live in more varied ways rather than sharing similar ways of living
Population pyramid	A bar chart representing the distribution of the population in different age groups
Post-industrial	The phase of society when manufacturing was the dominant part of the economy
Postmodernity/ postmodern	The era following modernity in which rationality becomes less important, image becomes more important and in which many old social divisions break down
Poverty	Lacking the resources to pay for the minimum acceptable lifestyle

Power	The ability of a person to get their own way or to determine outcomes regardless of the wishes of others
Pre-industrial society	Societies that existed before industrialization where most production was based upon agriculture
Primary relationships	The most important and emotionally charged personal relationships, e.g. between parents and children
Primary socialization	The first stage of the process through which children learn the culture of their society. This takes place in the family
Private enterprise	Businesses owned by individuals or shareholders rather than run by the state
Pull factors	Factors attracting international migrants to move to a particular country
Push factors	Factors encouraging international emigrants to leave a particular country
Radical feminism	The most extreme version of **feminism** which tends to see society as being completely dominated by men and sees the interests of men and women as being very different
Rationality	Behaviour which is geared towards achieving specified goals rather than based on emotion
Reconstituted family	A family that includes members from previous families which have broken up but which come together as two new partners form a relationship
Reflexive project of self	The way individuals constantly think about improving their own lives and developing their identity in contemporary society
Relative poverty	Lacking the resources to pay for a lifestyle which is deemed the minimum acceptable when compared with other people in a particular society at a particular time
Reproductive function	The function of the family in ensuring children are reproduced to enable the survival of society
Ruling class	In Marxist theory, the group who are dominant in society by virtue of their wealth and power
Sandbanham husband	In Nayar society, a visiting husband, usually a warrior. Each woman can have several of these husbands
Secularization	The process whereby religious thinking and religious institutions lose social significance
Separation	A couple living apart without getting divorced. Some separations are legal and formal, but most are not
Sexual function	The function of the family in controlling sexual behaviour through monogamy
Single-person household	A person living on their own
Social construction	A behaviour or practice which is produced by society even though it may seem natural or biological
Social mobility	The movement of people between social groups, especially social classes
Socialization	The process through which a person learns the culture of their society
Stabilization of adult personalities	To Parsons, the role of the family in maintaining the psychological health of adults by providing warmth and security and allowing them to act out childish elements in their personality

Status	The amount of esteem in which people are held by others in society
Stepfamily	A family which includes one or more children from a previous relationship
Subject class	In Marxist theory, the group in society who are dominated by the **ruling class** whom they have to work for because they lack the property to produce goods for themselves. The subject class are exploited by the **ruling class**
Super-diversity (of migration)	The increasingly varied nature of migrant groups with different nationalities and legal **statuses**
Superstructure	In Marxist theory, the non-economic parts of society such as the family which are shaped by the economy and controlled by the **ruling class**
Surplus value	Profits made by the **ruling class**
Surrogate motherhood	Where a woman gives birth to a child even though the child is not her genetic offspring (through in vitro fertilization)
Symmetrical family	A family in which both husband and wife do paid employment and both do some housework and provide childcare
Tali husband	In **Nayar** society, a husband who does not live with his wife or have a significant relationship with her
Triple shift	According to Duncombe and Marsden, the three types of work which create a burden for women: paid work, domestic work and **emotion work**
Underclass	The lowest social class, below the rest of the class structure, often seen as consisting of those reliant upon state benefits
Universal	Found in all societies
Values	General beliefs about what is right or wrong in a particular society
Visiting relationship	A relationship where an adult has a partner but they do not live together
Welfare state	Agencies run or financed by the government to provide for the well-being of members of society, such as education, the health service and social services
Working class	People who do manual jobs which require relatively few qualifications and are usually less well-paid than **middle class** jobs